MW01243731

403

THE FIVE FOSTERS

To Sherry and John,
Two wonderful people
Best wishes!
Betty Escapule
2007

by

Betty Foster Escapule

First Edition
First Printing, May, 2007

Betty Escapule
Book 464 of 1,000

Published by
B & C Enterprises
P.O. Box 453
Tombstone, AZ 85638

Printed by
Skyline Printing
Tucson, Arizona

This book is dedicated to my wonderful husband
and to my children and my siblings
for their encouragement and support - also to a terrific man
named Keith who convinced me it was all possible.

TABLE OF CONTENTS

PART ONE

PART TWO

PART THREE

PART FOUR

PART FIVE

PART ONE

The Beginning

This is the story of my first life - before I was married. It influenced me and prepared me for my second life. I learned how to work hard, sacrifice, laugh and most of all to love.

This first life was a wonderful life. It was unique. I owe so much to my father, mother, sister and brothers - and my stepmother.

Dad believed in the old saying about sleeping dogs and relatives - it's better to leave them alone. We knew we had kin but Dad preferred to live life simply - uncluttered by relatives. He did tell us though that if we met another Foster to ask them if they were related to the "Five Fosters" back in England. If they were, we were related. He never told us why the "Five Fosters" were noteworthy so that remained a mystery. Dad was the second or third generation over from England.

Our father basically raised us kids. Our mother was so young he treated her very much like he did us kids. Then after she was gone, he had the sole care of us. Later when he remarried, our stepmother stayed very much in the background. Dad was very strict and I think we were all a little afraid of him.

Dad was gone most of the time working so actually us kids raised each other. As a result we were close to each other not only in age but also emotionally.

The following is a collection of experiences seen mostly from my point of observation.

One of the guests at the Circle Z Ranch made this sketch of Dad.
1936

Dad

My father was a cowboy born in 1898, near Big Springs, Texas. He was the oldest of three brothers and he had six older sisters. They lived in a remote area where there was no school. His father waited until the youngest child was old enough to start school then he moved the family to town and put all nine children in the first grade. Shortly thereafter he died from typhoid.

Dad was nine years old and big for his age. He quit school without having learned to read or write and went to work for a farmer to help support his family. He was given room and board and paid a dollar a day. If the weather was bad he didn't get paid. When he was in his mid-teens a couple of cowboys came through town. They told him cowboys were paid thirty dollars a month with room and board and the weather didn't affect their pay. I guess he figured cowpunching was a lot more fun than farming so he left Texas and came to Arizona.

Sometime during his youth he was snowbound in a cabin for the winter with an old man. Dad was bored and wanted the old man to talk to him but the old man wanted to read. He told Dad to teach himself to read and write so he did. He had a beautiful handwriting but the use of capital letters and punctuation eluded him. He did math in his head and he used a series of knots tied in a piggin' string for larger numbers and problems.

Dad drove a twenty mule team ore wagon in Tombstone. We had a picture of him standing by the front wheel of the wagon wearing a white ten-gallon hat in front of the Bird Cage Theater.

Sadly this picture has been lost.

It was while he was in Tombstone that he met Sheriff Harry Wheeler - actually he put him in jail. They talked through the night. Dad thought a lot of this sheriff and years later he named a promising young horse Harry Wheeler.

Later he homesteaded in Patagonia. There he married a woman twenty years his senior. This marriage didn't last too long. He wound up living in the barn and she lived in the house. He gave her everything when they split up.

When Dad was thirty five he met and married our mother. (1934) She was fifteen and the youngest of six children. My sister, Mary was born the next year, (1935) Sammy nineteen months later (1937) and then after another thirteen months Bailey and I came along - twins. (1938) There were two years and eight months between the four of us.

Dad was the foreman at the Circle Z Guest Ranch when Mary and Sammy were born. While F. J. Frost was a guest there he said this about Dad, "Sam is a composite of all the types of real cowboys I have ever known."

Later he cowboyed for the Hershel Ranch in the San Rafael Valley and that's where Bailey and I joined the family.

Dad was a philosopher and humorist. He had a deep love of horses, game chickens and hounds.

Dad and his hounds.

Dad with a lead horse and a pack mule.

Dad on a Steel Dust quarter horse named Simon Dick.

Dad and Mom when they were first married.

Dad and a hound sitting in the doorway of his cabin in Patagonia.

Mom with a hound pup in front of the cabin.

Dad with a corral of horses at the Circle Z.

Mary and Dad.

Daddy holding Sammy at the Circle Z.

Early Memories

These are some of my earliest recollections. Ours was a happy family with lots of fun and laughter. We loved our parents and they loved us. Life was good.

Every morning Dad was up early and built a fire in the big wood heater in the living room. At five o'clock in the morning he called, "Come a-running!" And we did. The boys on side of the stove and Mary and I on the other where we got dressed. We were very modest. From the time we could walk we got up at five in the morning and "came a-running". As soon as we were called our feet hit the floor.

We were happy children - well disciplined and well behaved. Dad had a theory. He figured we all had average intelligence and normal hearing, therefore, we should obey after being told once. Clearly we heard him and understood what he said so once was sufficient. Punishment was swift and thorough. His other theory was punishment should be severe enough that we tried not to be repeat offenders if possible. Now this may sound harsh but it wasn't. He loved us and was very fair.

Once Dad told us not to climb on top of the barn roof so I didn't. But Mary, Sammy and Bailey did just that. Immediately I ran to Dad and informed him. He went to the corner of the barn and called the other kids to come down. As each one came down he gave them a very hard spanking. I stood by and watched, proud of my good behavior. When the last kid had been spanked Dad turned and picked me up and gave me twice the spanking the others had gotten. Then he told me that was for tattling.

One time when Mom was trying to get dinner on the table I was so hungry I didn't think I could wait any longer so I begged and begged until I got a biscuit. Mom told me to eat it in the kitchen and not to tell the other kids. So, of course, the first thing I did as soon as Mom turned her back was run into the living room and show the other kids my biscuit.

No sooner did I show them the biscuit that I felt Mom's long arm of the law pick me up. That was a spanking to remember.

Me in a walker.

Mary holding me up.

Housing

We didn't have the conveniences people have today. We never had electricity and seldom indoor plumbing or water in the house. When asked if we had running water Dad always said yes - you ran and got it and it was us kids that ran and got it. We cooked on wood stoves and heated with wood. We were comfortable and we were clean. There was always plenty of water because there was water for the livestock. We put the wash tub on the wood stove and filled it with water. When it was warm, it took two of us to lift it off the stove and set it on the floor. We closed the kitchen door and bathed in the kitchen. Then two of us carried the tub outside and emptied it. Mary and I worked together for our baths and the boys worked together for theirs.

We kept a teakettle and coffee pot on the stove. As soon as a meal was cooked the enamelware dishpans were filled with water and set on the stove to heat while we ate. If the water wasn't quite hot enough we added some from the teakettle. Mary and I took turns washing and drying the dishes. The cast iron skillets were turned upside down on the wood stove to dry so they wouldn't rust. We usually had a table at the end of the stove. This served as a work surface. We kept a large covered bucket or pot filled with water and a ladle or tin cup beside it. This was almost as good as running water. Washing up was done outside at a small table with an enamelware wash basin, bar of soap and towel. Outhouses were set a distance from the house. These were kept swept out and a bucket of ashes from the wood stove sat in the corner with a small shovel. You sprinkled some ashes down the hole before you left. A Sears Roebuck catalog served as paper. Most outhouses had black widow spiders under the seat but as far as I know, no one was ever bitten. They stayed back in the corners and we left them alone.

Dad had a very realistic ceramic rattlesnake that he kept in the outhouse. This surprised and startled our guests. When we moved, the snake moved with us.

Some of the houses were screened and if not there were plenty of fly swatters. We always had a gunny sack cooler. This kept our milk, butter and eggs cool. We usually had chickens of some sort but we didn't always have a regular milk cow. Quite often our milk cow was a range cow that had a big bag and enough milk for her calf and some for us. When Dad found such a cow she was brought home and broke to milk. This provided us with enough milk to make cornbread, biscuits, gravy and maybe some to drink.

Some of the houses we lived in were pretty primitive. Mom flattened cardboard boxes and lined the inside of this one house to keep out the cold wind. No wonder this place was referred to as the Crack House. I remember one house or maybe several that had aging wallpaper that hung loosely from the walls with strings of cheesecloth hanging down. Although I was small I vowed never to live in a house with wallpaper in it when I grew up and I never did.

We even lived in one house with a dirt floor. I remember Mom giving me a cup of water and when I drank what I wanted, I crawled under the table and poured the rest of the water on the floor - after all it was dirt. My mother pulled me out from under the table and tanned my hide. It seems you didn't pour water on the floor even it was just a dirt floor. Mom kept the floor dampened and swept clean.

We may have been patched but we were always clean, our hair

combed, our clothes ironed and our house clean. It seemed like times were always hard.

No matter how primitive our dwelling was it was home and filled with love. The one thing I remember most about my early childhood was that we were happy.

Learning to Ride

We began riding at a very early age. Dad put a horse shoe on the horn of his saddle and covered it with rawhide. This made an ideal seat for a baby or small child. As soon as we were old enough to sit up he took us for short rides.

By the time Bailey and I were two we rode with Mom and Dad every other day. Bailey sat behind Mom and held onto her belt and I sat behind Dad and held onto the end of the belt on his chaps. We sat on the skirt of the saddle and were careful not to touch the horse. Most of Dad's horses weren't very gentle and didn't like to be touched off of the saddle.

The next day it would be Mary's and Sammy's turn to ride. So every other day two of us rode with Mom and Dad and the other two stayed at the Mexican's house.

Sammy was just learning to talk and he spoke Spanish before he did English. Sammy didn't talk at home. If he wanted something he grunted and pointed at it. All was well until one day when Mom went to pick up Mary and Sammy. There was Sammy sitting on the Mexican woman's lap speaking Spanish - patting her face and calling her "Mama". Mom was jealous. That ended our staying with this family. We grew up very comfortable on the back of a horse.

Candy

L ike all kids we loved candy but there wasn't much of it around. Once in a while someone made fudge. That was really good even if it was grainy or "spoon fudge" that was under cooked and didn't quite harden. Of course, there was taffy. When company came over, the grown-ups made taffy. Everybody got involved - even us kids. The taffy was cooked and poured into a large buttered platter to cool. Clean flour sacks were laid out on the table. The edges of the taffy were pulled toward the center and as soon as it cooled enough not to cause blisters, everyone buttered their hands and the taffy pulling began. It was still too hot to hold, so it was passed and pulled from person to person very quickly. Even us kids were given small pieces to pull.

There was lots of laughing and everyone had fun. When the taffy turned white it was pulled into a rope and laid on the flour sacks. Then it was hit with the back of a table knife and broken into pieces. We all ate as much of the warm taffy as we wanted.

Bailey and I found what we thought was chocolate candy. Actually, it was a box of Exlax. It was always share and share alike, so we divided it and ate the whole box.

Dad had remodeled the outhouse and built a low seat with two holes for Bailey and I. We were about two years old and we wore one piece denim jumpers with the drop seats. We were very modest. Each of us would close our eyes while the other one got seated. Then we sat and visited. We spent a lot of time in that outhouse. To this day neither of us like chocolate.

Bailey and me at Grandma's house.

Bailey and me sitting on an empty dynamite box.

Sammy and Bailey getting milk for the cats.

Bailey and the Catfish

We lived at the Stone House near St. David for awhile. This was one of the camps on Boquillas. There was a cienega there which is sort of a marsh from artesian water. Also there was a dirt tank (earthen dam) not too far from the house. In the evenings we fished in this tank for catfish. Sammy and Mary caught fish but I don't think I ever caught anything. Bailey was the fisherman in the family. He enjoyed it more than the rest of us even if he just caught mud turtles. But he did catch fish too.

One day someone came by with a tank on the back of their pickup and it had catfish in it. This was a long tank lying on it's side with a hole on top with a lid. Bailey and I couldn't have been more than three years old. When Bailey heard there were fish in the tank we went outside for a look. We climbed onto the tank and lifted the lid. The smell was awful but we didn't care. It was dark in there and we couldn't see anything so we helped each other and dropped down inside this dark smelly tank. We didn't think about how deep the water was but it only came above our knees. Then the fun began. We chased some pretty big catfish around in the tank. There were lots of them in there. Finally we caught one and we got stuck by it's fins. That ended our fishing. We were no match for these fish and we helped each other out of the tank.

Bailey and me.

Mary and Sammy.

Lupe

D ad always had his game chickens but they didn't lay too many eggs so Mom had a flock of laying hens. She had just raised a bunch of white leghorn pullets up to laying size when a neighbor came by. She had a young donkey not yet broken to ride and wanted to trade him for the pullets. The deal was made and we had a donkey. Sammy had a girl friend named Lupe so he named the donkey Lupe.

We gentled and broke the donkey just by the sheer force of numbers. We really loved this little black donkey. When Dad drove the mule wagon we took turns riding Lupe and he trotted along behind the wagon. And when Dad rode horseback he put one of us on the donkey. He got a lot of use. When we moved to the Wolf Place from the Stone House, Lupe went with us. Bailey and I turned four years old there and that summer we met Mom's father, Grandpa, for the first time. All of us loved him. He made little rhymes for us. Mine was "Betty, my little queen, will you have a little bean?" We washed his feet, combed his hair and showered him with attention. Then he left us. He went to Patagonia to visit family. There he had a heart attack and died.

The Bakarichs lived about five miles west of us. Mrs. Bakarich was a widow with eight children - the last two about our ages. Mom raised a big garden that year in spite of the Johnson grass. She would tie two gunny sacks together and fill them with vegetables and water melons and throw them over the donkey's back. We would leave home early in the morning and go to the Bakarichs for the day. Mom, Sammy and Mary would walk and

Bailey and I rode on Lupe's back with the vegetables. We would make it back home before supper time.

When we left the Wolf Place we gave Lupe to the Bakarichs and when we returned years later they gave him back.

Lupe was a good donkey. He didn't neck reign but he was easy to handle, gentle, had a good disposition and was never lazy. With a slight nudge he would break into a lope or a run if you wanted him to. Best of all he could single-foot. This is a gait that is faster than a walk and almost as fast as a trot - very smooth - with only one foot touching the ground at a time. He loved cornbread and begged at the yard gate with a long , loud bray. Everyone , even Mom, would stop what we were doing to give Lupe his cornbread. Without a doubt this was the best donkey any of us had ever seen.

Cousin Nadine, Betty, Bailey, Sammy and Mary in the San Pedro River...Thursday crossing at the Wolf Place.

Learning to Read

We all loved Mom and wanted to spend as much time as possible in her lap. The one sure way to do this was to read to her. Bailey and I taught ourselves to read so we could sit in Mom's lap. By the time we were four we were good readers and we could write too.

We were living near Sonoita. When it came time for school to start there weren't enough children to open the school. The teacher came to the house and asked if she could have Bailey and me. We could already read and write so we started the first grade when we were four. We wouldn't be five until February. School opened that year but the teacher wasn't too happy with Bailey and me as we couldn't stay awake all day.

PART TWO

California

We left the Wolf Place and moved to Sonoita and from there we went to California where Dad worked in the oil fields.

There were a few good memories. The four of us kids had walked down the little dirt road to the main road to wait for Dad to come home from work. While we were waiting we decided to throw rocks at the next car that came by. We were country kids but we knew better.

Well, here came a car and we pelted it with rocks. To our surprise it turned in on our road and drove up to the house. A man got out and went to the door. We just knew he was going to tell Mom on us but he didn't. He was our Uncle Bailey. This was the only time we saw Uncle Bailey and then only for a day. He was in the army.

Mary and I had a yellow cat that let us dress him in doll clothes and feed him a bottle while we pushed him in a buggy. I can remember Dad bringing me home a little rabbit in his lunch box. And I can remember laying in field of cool, fresh alfalfa in bloom. But there were other memories too.

As far as we knew we were still a happy family. Then on Christmas Eve while Dad was working the night shift Mom left. She loaded us kids and our Christmas presents into the car and dropped us off at her sister's house. It would be a long time before we saw her again and never again would we be the family we once were. This was something between our parents and they kept it away from us kids. We never saw them quarrel. The one thing we were sure of was that Mom and Dad loved us.

We saw our mother only once after she dropped us off and then only for about an hour. She was very sick. Our lives were chaotic and our future uncertain.

We were playing out in the front yard at Aunt Mary's house when Dad pulled up to the curb. He didn't get out of the car but called us kids over and told us to get in. Grandma was standing in front of the house and she grabbed Bailey and held on to him. She knew Dad wouldn't leave as long as she held one of us back. But sweet, gentle Bailey surprised Grandma. When he couldn't struggle and get free he began kicking and hitting until he was too much for Grandma and he managed to get loose and run to the car and get in. He wasn't going to be left. As soon as we were all in the car Dad drove off before anyone could stop him.

The car was a coupe with one seat. Dad had taken the lid of the trunk off, turned it sideways and secured it to the taillights with baling wire. He put a couple of quilts down on the floor of the trunk and made a "nest" for us kids.

Dad had picked us up about midmorning. I don't remember him stopping even once. Either we traveled a long way or Dad was a slow driver - probably some of both. We watched it get dark. It was a clear winter night and lots of stars. We snuggled up together and kept warm hidden from the world. We felt safe and happy. We were with Dad and he would take care of us. We stayed curled up on the floor of the trunk never looking out until the car stopped.

Dad had taken us to a cousin's house close to the railroad tracks. They were a couple with older children. The woman made dinner for us - fried chicken with mashed potatoes and gravy. Later that night we boarded the train.

Anyway, Dad saw an attorney and legally kidnapped us as custody hadn't been settled. So with just the clothes on our backs we caught a train and came back to Arizona. I was five years old.

Dad didn't have any family he was close to. All he had was us kids. With Mom gone Dad was determined to raise us kids and keep us from being separated. And he did. I'm sure it wasn't easy, not back in those days, and not with us so young. He did raise us and he did keep us together as a family.

Great Aunt Ida

Aunt Ida was Grandma's sister on our mother's side. These two sisters were as different as day and night. Aunt Ida was stern but she liked us and was good to us and good to Dad. It was to her house that we came when we first arrived back from California. Dad went back to work at the Circle Z Guest Ranch west of Patagonia and left us kids at Aunt Ida's.

Aunt Ida lived outside of Patagonia down a dirt road and across a sand wash. She kept goats. One of the first things we did was put Sammy on the old billy goat. We didn't want him to get bucked off so we tied his feet together under the billy goat's belly and he held on to the goat's horns. Then we turned the goat loose and Sammy went for a wild ride all over the place. Aunt Ida came out and rescued her goat and that was the last of the goat riding.

However, there were lot's of burros that ran along the sand wash. All the local kids rode these burros until they were bucked off or scraped off. So this entertained us and kept us busy.

I was in the livingroom alone one day and for some strange reason not even known to me I decided to climb the drapes which hung from the ceiling to the floor. When I was about halfway up, the curtain rod pulled loose from the wall and I landed on the floor under the drapes. In came Aunt Ida and she was not too pleased with me.

Then at dinner one time I couldn't eat my beans. They were too hot. So I crumbled my crackers onto the beans but this didn't

41

help much. Next I poured my milk into my plate. This cooled off the beans but now I had slop and I didn't want to eat it. Aunt Ida never said a word, she just took my plate off the table. I was releived but at supper that night she set my plate of beans, crackers and milk in front of me. I ate it because I somehow knew I wouldn't get anything else to eat until I cleaned my plate.

At night we knelt beside our bed and said our prayers. We said "Now I lay me down to sleep" followed by God bless everybody and everything we could think of. In came Aunt Ida. She asked us if that was the only prayer we knew. It was. So then she taught us the Lord's Prayer. Aunt Ida was a good woman. There was a radio about the size of a small dresser in the livingroom. When the news came on we all had to be very quiet. Everyone gathered around the radio and listened to the war news. We heard President Roosevelt and Winston Churchill. We felt the gravity of the war. Shoes, tires, gasoline, meat and sugar were rationed. Tin cans were washed and their lids put inside and flattened. Any scrap metal that could be found was gathered for the scrap man who came by on Thursdays. Everybody including children did everything they could for the war effort. We were all patriots.

We left Aunt Ida's and moved to Gardner Canyon where Dad went to work for Dink Parker taking care of his race horses. That's where we were living when we heard the war had ended.

Patagonia

We walked from Aunt Ida's house to Patagonia. Then we went up the hill on the other side to go to school. Bailey and I were in the second grade. The second grade was in a small building off by itself. It was one room and heated by a wood heater in the back of the room.

One morning a boy named Dos threw a handful of .22 shells into the stove when the teacher wasn't looking. The shells began exploding. When it was all over the stove lids had been blown off and there were lots of holes in the chimney. Nothing caught fire and no one was hurt but Dos was in trouble. Bailey and I always took care of each other even at school. I worried about Bailey and I wanted to help him with his work. I was always over at his desk. The teacher's remedy for this was to put Bailey back in the first grade. This was the first time we had been separated and it was hard on both of us. I don't know why the teacher didn't just punish me.

The Maypole

On the playground at the school in Patagonia was a Maypole. This was the first and last one I ever saw. It was a tall steel pole with a wheel on top with chains hanging down with rings to hold on to. The kids held on to the rings and ran as fast as they could around the Maypole. When they could run no faster everyone lifted up their feet and centrifugal force carried them high in the air and around and around they went. It looked like the most fun thing I could imagine but when I wanted a turn the big kids said I was too small. They wouldn't let me play on the Maypole so I just stood back and watched and wished.

I stayed after school one day until everyone went home and I had the Maypole to myself. I could barely reach the rings but I did manage to hold on to one. I ran as fast as I could on my tiptoes and around and around I went. I picked up my feet and was lifted high in the air. What I didn't realize was that I was too light to make the wheel at the top turn so when I picked up my feet, the wheel stopped. Around and around the Maypole I went with the chains wrapping me around the pole. Higher and higher I was twisted around the Maypole. Finally I came to a stop, twisted and tangled high above the ground. I couldn't get untangled and I couldn't hold on. Down I went like a rock on the rough concrete base holding the Maypole. I landed on my face, knees, elbows, hands, arms and legs. I had a lot of bare skin that was torn up.

Bleeding and hurt I picked myself up off the ground and limped back to Aunt Ida's house and home to Mary. Mary was not only my sister and best friend, she was the closest thing I had to a mother. Mary comforted me, cleaned me up and doctored my wounds. I never went near the Maypole again.

Gardner Canyon

Dad went to work for Dink Parker in Gardner Canyon near Sonoita. We went to a little one room school house in the middle of nowhere. The bus driver wouldn't drive up the canyon where we lived so we boarded with Bill Douglas, an old friend of Dad's who lived further down the canyon. He had two girls in school and the bus picked them up.

This bus driver was pretty independent. He wouldn't take us all the way to school either but dropped us off at the gate. The school was probably another half mile. We would all take our shoes off line them up, crawl under the fence and walk to school barefoot.

It was at this school that Sammy got "married" for the first time. He loved the girls and always had a girlfriend. One day during recess we gathered all the petals off the white thistles. Someone played preacher and preformed the ceremony and we showered the couple with white petals. It was a beautiful fairy tale wedding.

Bailey had a girlfriend too. She was the younger Douglas girl, Dorothy. She was a pretty little redhead.

Bill Douglas had a dairy and one of the fun things to do was grab a cow's tail while she was running. You held on tight and ran as fast as you could to keep from falling. She pulled you along making you take giant leaps behind her. This was called riding the cow's tail.

Dorothy grabbed a cow by the tail and instead of running she kicked Dorothy breaking her leg. The rest of us would go off to

47

play but Dorothy was in a cast and had to stay behind. Bailey would either stay with her or bring her back a flower or pretty rock.

We moved a lot and the years went by. When Bailey was old enough he married Dorothy.

Naco

For a short time we lived in the Naco area while Dad worked in the mines. We walked to school and if we took the short cut across country we had to cross several barbed wire fences on the way to town. There were stiles on these fences. These were the first and last stiles I ever saw. A stile is a set of steps that go up and over a fence. I think these were for the ladies when they used to wear long dresses and couldn't very well crawl through or roll under a barbed wire fence.

Naco was a small town on the Mexican border with a small school. At recess time all the kids had to play baseball from the first grade to the eighth. I was only seven and I had never heard of baseball. When sides were picked I was the last one chosen. Of course, I struck out every time it was my turn to bat. Because of this the other kids hated me and I hated baseball.

One morning during class the boys were giving the teacher a hard time. One boy would raise his hand and ask to be excused to go to the bathroom. As soon as he got back another boy would raise his hand and ask to be excused and so on.

Well, it seems that Dad had decided Bailey needed a laxative so at bedtime he gave him some Exlax. The next morning when Bailey raised his hand just as another boy returned from the bathroom, the teacher had just about enough of that game. She told Bailey it was only a few minutes until recess and he could wait. Bailey had to wait but the Exlax couldn't and didn't. Mary was summoned from class and told to take Bailey home and clean him up. That had to be a long walk home.

I think we were all glad when Dad went back to cowboying and we left Naco behind.

Scratching Mary

Like all kids we were forbidden to fight with each other. I don't remember what the fight was over but Mary and I were really going at it. I was much smaller than Mary so it wasn't surprising that I was getting the worst of it.

I knew better than to scratch or bite but somehow in the heat of battle I forgot. I scratched Mary on the forearm. It was self defense, of course. Suddenly there was blood running down her arm. When I saw the blood I knew that I had scratched Mary much worse than I had intended but the damage was done. Mary would carry the scars from this for the rest of her life.

Dad didn't always whip us when we misbehaved. He had a sense of justice. He called me over and told me to sit down. I didn't know what he was going to do but I knew I was in real trouble. Dad took out his pocket knife which was always razor sharp and without a word he cut off my fingernails down to the quick. Then he sent me to my room to think about the terrible thing I had done.

I went to my room and I did think about what I had done and how awful it was but I also thought about how lucky it was that I didn't bite Mary.

It would be a long time until my fingernails grew back. I had learned my lesson. Never again would I use my fingernails for a weapon.

Guns

Guns were a natural part of our lives. As far back as I can remember Dad kept a loaded 30-30 behind the kitchen door. He said that was in case a coyote came around to get one of his chickens. We always had a dog and it was his job to keep the varmints away from the house. Anyway we never saw Dad use the 30-30.

Dad also kept a loaded six shooter in the table by his bed. He had a table with a deep compartment that the front panel opened up on. Inside this table he kept his True Detective magazines and the six shooter. At night he laid the six shooter on top of the table and in the morning he put it away again. Whenever we moved the table moved with us. It was homemade and sturdy. I think Dad probably made it. He always kept it beside his bed as a night stand and on top was a lamp and an ashtray.

He left us kids alone all the time with these two loaded guns in the house. He had a theory about guns. Leave them loaded and they would be left alone. It was an empty gun that invited inspection. I think there was a lot of wisdom in that. We saw these guns as something very dangerous and we left them alone. We were never tempted to touch them.

The Sands Ranch

We lived at the headquarters and caught the school bus at the Whetstone Junction. The foreman's wife, Polly, drove us to and from the junction. We went to school in Tombstone in the old two- storey yellow school house. The building was so old no one was allowed upstairs as it was considered unsafe.

One day Sammy's teacher, Miss Giacoma, noticed he had a lot of little red bumps and suspected chicken pox so she took him down to the town doctor. After examining Sammy he said all he had were mosquito bites and he was returned to school.

Well, Sammy infected the whole school and the school had to be closed. We were all sent home and the Health Department put a quarantine sign on the front door. Strangely, I never did get the chicken pox.

Dad was gone all day so we were left alone alot. The left over biscuits or cornbread were put in a white tin bread box and we were allowed to eat these if we were hungry. We would fill our pockets with bread and leave for the day. We were like little nomads - always on the move.

We knew where all the windmills and stock tanks were and these provided us with water. There was always a tin cup on a baling wire at the windmills and we would catch clean water fresh from the well if the wind was blowing. If not we drank from the watering trough where the cows drank. We blew away any debris on the surface and strained the water through our teeth. We didn't want to swallow any water bugs.

Not having gum a choice item to chew was hardened tar
we chipped out of an old empty stock tank. It was quite tastey.
Another favorite was a piece of cow salt broken off the salt blocks
that were put out for the cattle. Of course, the very best was
mesquite honey. This was hardened sugared sap found on the
mesquite trees. It was delicious. You had to be careful when
chewing this as it could stick your teeth together and you couldn't
get your mouth open until the sap softened. When you finally
were able to get your teeth apart it felt like they were going to be
pulled out by the roots. What fun!

Sammy and Bailey liked to imagine themselves as Indians
and always had a teepee somewhere in the limestone hills. The
teepee was made of yucca poles and gunny sacks, held together
with baling wire. If I wanted to play I had to be the squaw and
carry the yucca poles and gunny sacks from place to place.
Sammy didn't like to stay in one place very long so there was a
lot of carrying to do. While the boys set up the teepee I gathered
rocks for the fire pit and built a fire. Even though we weren't very
old we were allowed to carry matches and build fires. I think the
fun was in the setting up and tearing down of the teepee.

At eight years old Dad considered us old enough to carry
a rifle, a single shot .22. We didn't load the gun until we saw a
rabbit. We ate what we shot.

When Sammy turned eight years old Dad brought home a
4-10 shotgun for him. We were always supposed to hunt alone for
safety reasons. Dad was gone and Sammy went hunting with the
shotgun. Bailey and I went with him. Sammy shot a dove with
the first shot. My job as squaw was to retrieve the dead dove,
pick it, clean it and cook it. The teepee was some distance and we
set off in a slow trot. When we got there I built a fire and cooked
the dove. I thought I had done a pretty good job. But Sammy
informed me I should have gotten some salt when we passed

54

a salt block.

I don't remember riding horses at the Sands Ranch. If we wanted to go somewhere we traveled on foot over long distances and we were always on the move. We never stayed home. Later Dad said he would see our tracks miles and miles from home. He never worried about us. We spent most of our time outside. The thought of getting lost didn't enter our minds. We always just knew where we were and how to get home.

There was one time I do remember riding. There had been a big rain and the dirt tank was full of muddy water. Dad took us four kids there on horseback and let us swim our horses in the dirt tank. Of course, Bailey and I couldn't swim and I'm not sure if Mary and Sammy could at that time.

We pulled the saddles off our horses and rode bareback into the water. I was afraid of the water but on the back of a horse I felt safe. I was surprised - as the horse began to swim only his head was out of the water stretched out on the surface. The water came up around my waist. That was the only time I swam a horse. We all had a lot of fun that day.

PART THREE

The Rooster

Fort Huachuca was closed and Dad took a job as guard at the gate. We lived at a place called the Slash Z. It was located on the bombing range northeast of Fort Huachuca. There was a large empty two story building down the hill close to the barn and corrals. On top of the hill was a large burnt adobe house with a fireplace in every room, a large glassed-in porch and a walled-in patio with an outside staircase leading up to the roof. There were two small separate burnt adobe buildings. These had been the maid's and butler's quarters. Mary and I stayed in the maid's quarters, Dad in the butler's quarters and Sammy and Bailey in the big house.

On his way to work Dad would drop us off on the highway near the North Gate at McCrea City. There was nothing there but the ruins of a few houses. We would wait for the big yellow school bus to take us to school in Tombstone. After school the bus would drop us off again at McCrea City and we would wait for Dad to pick us up on his way home from work.

We were always up by five in the morning. Dad didn't have an alarm clock so he built a small stand, put some newspapers under it, sat it on the floor of his room by the bed and every night he caught the game rooster and put him on the stand. The rooster always crowed at five in the morning and then having done his job was put outside. Dad was never late for work and we never missed the bus thanks to this rooster.

Dad had a real love of game chickens. He never named the hens but all the roosters were named Ceasar.

Mary's Housekeeping

Mary and I did the dishes and most of the cooking. We all took care of our bedrooms but it was Mary's job to keep the rest of the house clean. Dad expected a clean house. When he came home from work the house was always neat and the floors swept.

There was a rug in the living room and one day Dad decided to look under the rug. He suspicioned something was not as it should be. It seems Mary had been sweeping everything under the rug. That was it! The house was going to get a good cleaning.

The house was burnt adobe with cement floors. All of us were put to work. We packed everything out of the house and carried it out into the yard. Then Dad brought the water hose in the house and washed it down from floor to ceiling even the windows. Then all of us swept the water out of the house and let it dry. Next everything was moved back in. What a difference that made! Now we had a really clean house and it stayed clean for a long time. And that's how a cowboy cleans house.

The Bribe

From spending so much time alone and on our own we formed a government. We were tribal. Mary was chief. She became our judge and our punisher but she was accountable to Dad. If we made cookies or whatever we had it was divided four ways. It was share and share alike. On decisions it was one vote per person and each vote carried the same weight.

And so it was that one day Sammy transgressed and needed punishing - but he ran. None of us had done this before. The chase was on! Through the house, down the hill, over the corral fence and finally on top of the rusty barn roof where it all came to an end. The roof gave way and Sammy fell to the ground below where Mary caught him.

Bailey and I followed the chase and watched in disbelief as Mary sat astraddle of Sammy choking him. Blood came out of his nose and mouth. Mary was horrified by what she had done. So she picked up Sammy - she was amazingly strong for her size - and carried him up the hill to the big house. Then she washed him up, examined him and decided he would be alright. But there was a problem. She was accountable to Dad. So, of course, the political thing to do was to bribe the witnesses.

In a large white enamelware pot, Mary made a double batch of vanilla pudding. Chocolate wouldn't do as Bailey and I didn't like chocolate after our fiasco with Exlax. She gave each of us a spoon and carried the white pot of hot vanilla pudding into the large bathroom and shut and locked the door. There was no one for miles around but she was taking no chances. Then Mary put the lid down on the toilet and set the pot down. We all knelt down with our spoon around the toilet and took a vow of silence and ate the pudding.

Dad working as guard at the Main Gate at Fort Huachuca.

Hog Tying the Cat

Dad was working as guard at Fort Huachuca over at the West Gate. He only worked days because of us kids and he was allowed to take us to work if he had to work holidays or weekends. It was the weekend and Dad let me bring a half grown kitten along to play with.

We had already "branded" all the dogs and cats with scissors and they didn't seem to mind. I think they liked the attention. But I was ready to move on to something else. I decided to practice hog tying on this kitten. I couldn't find anything to tie him up with - no rope or string - but I did find a spool of thread. I tied the thread around a front leg, then laid this leg on his hind legs and tied him up hard and fast.

Of course, in due time the kitten wanted free so I tried to untie him but the thread had completely disappeared into his fur. Then he began to howl and bite. Dad came running and although we thought Dad could do just about anything, freeing that cat really put him to the test. He didn't take too kindly to being bitten. I was bitten quite a few times too but I didn't complain. I didn't get spanked but I did get a good scolding. Hog tying the cat was definitely off limits.

A Bear in the House

There was a dance at Fletcher's Roundup every Saturday night. Dad worked as deputy sheriff at these dances leaving us kids alone at night. But it was only one night a week and we were out in the country out of harms way.

One night I heard something in the house. It was making lots of noise - growling and snarling. I woke up Mary. She heard it too. Sometimes it was quiet but then it would breathe real loud - then more growling and snarling. We decided we should go get the boys.

Dad was gone and we were home alone. The boys listened and the heard the same thing that Mary and I heard. We all decided it must be something big. The only thing we could think of was a bear. The more we listened the more sure we were that this had to be a bear. This thing was in Dad's room. We decided to open the door just a crack and have a look. Well, there lay Dad sound asleep and snoring. He had come home early. He was our bear.

The Stock Tank

Down the hill from the house was a windmill and a large deep cement stock tank completely full of water. It was hot and we were home alone. We decided to go swimming. Sammy and Mary could swim but Bailey and I couldn't. We each had a short piece of crosstie we could straddle and hold onto the edge of the tank. So far so good. We were all having lots of fun.

There was a heavy rope stretched across the middle of the tank. Pretty soon the other kids were going back and forth across the tank holding onto the rope - even Bailey without his crosstie. They wanted me to join the fun and cross the tank. Well, the rope was partly submerged in the water and covered with algae. It looked like it had been there a very long time. I was afraid the rope would break with me. They all showed me how strong the rope was. So finally I started across. About halfway across the rope did break and I sank like a rock.

Mary was a strong swimmer but she just froze and was no help. Sammy dived in after me. He was wearing blue swim trunks and I could see him coming to help me. I held on to him and tried to get to the surface but the water was too deep. All I succeeded in doing was holding Sammy down so he couldn't come up either. We were both drowning.

Dad wouldn't be home from work until evening. But for some strange reason he came home in the middle of the day. When he couldn't find us he ran down the hill to the stock tank. He jumped in the tank, clothes and all. I saw Dad coming towards us. First he pried my hands off Sammy and gave Sammy a push to the surface where he swam out. Then Dad swam with me to the edge. We were saved.

Later I saw Dad's wallet and papers spread out to dry. Even his boots were drying out. I really felt bad as I considered it my fault all this had happened but most of all I felt bad for nearly drowning Sammy when he tried to help me. I just hoped everything would dry and things would be alright again. But this wouldn't be my last time in that stock tank.

The Boats

It was a cold windy day in the middle of winter and Mary and I had each made a little boat. We took our boats down to the cement stock tank. We put our boats in the water and watched the wind blow them across the tank. We were standing on the top edge of the tank. In the excitement of watching our boats being blown across the water, I began jumping up and down. The next thing I knew I had jumped in. The water was so cold and so deep. Of course, I couldn't swim. I went down and came up in the middle of the tank. Mary could have jumped in and rescued me but the water was too cold. I went down and came up time after time sure I was going to drown. Finally I came up close enough to the edge for Mary to reach me with a piece of baling wire and pull me out.

She took me up to the house and took off my wet clothes. None of us had many clothes and that was the last of my clean clothes. Mary rolled me up in a blanket and carried me up on the flat roof. She laid me by the edge where there was a wall about a foot high. This broke the wind and the sun felt warm. Then Mary hung up my wet clothes to dry.

About this time the Bakarichs came over. All the kids were playing and the only thing I could do was to be very quiet up there on the roof, rolled up in my blanket with no clothes on. I didn't want anyone to know I was up there. I needn't have worried, Nobody even missed me.

Two Men in the Window

It had snowed earlier and there was several inches on the ground. There was a full moon and the night was almost as bright as day. It was so still. Then there was a noise outside and this woke up Bailey. He saw two men in the window. He was so scared and since you can't be scared by yourself he woke Sammy. None of us kids ever had a bed of our own. Mary and I slept together and the boys slept together.

Sammy and Bailey watched as the two men tried to get in the window. They were scratching on the screen and making quite a bit of noise but they didn't speak to each other. They seemed to be having some difficulty getting the screen off. The boys wanted to run to Dad's bedroom but they had to cross an open floor and could easily be seen from the window. So they just crouched down in their blankets and watched the two men working on the screen.

Toward morning the two men left without getting the window open. Then the boys woke up Dad. After daylight he took Sammy and Bailey outside to investigate. There under the window was a torn gunny sack and lots of tracks - mule tracks. It seems that during the night the two mules had gotten into the yard and were playing tug of war with the gunny sack. They had pushed and rubbed against the screen. The boys were laying in bed looking up at the window and couldn't see the mules' ears. All they could see were their heads and they really did look like two men.

The Blackbird

Christmas came and there was lots of snow on the ground. Times were hard. Dad didn't have anything to make for Christmas dinner so he took the shotgun and went down the hill to the corral. There in the snow was a flock of blackbirds. He shot and killed a bunch of them. I guess we were going to have "Four and twenty blackbirds baked into a pie". This was going to be our Christmas dinner.

Anyway us kids ran out and picked up the dead birds. The blackbird I picked up was still alive. After closer examination he only had a broken wing. He wasn't going to be part of our dinner. I patched up his wing and kept him in a cage until he healed. Dad put a band on his leg and I set him free. I was sure I would never see him again and I didn't.

One day Dad came home with an amazing story. He was on guard duty at the Main Gate that spring and out on the lawn was a flock of blackbirds. There among them was my blackbird still wearing his leg band.

Since then the blackbird has been my favorite bird. I have been fortunate enough to have two other very special blackbirds in my life.

Buddy and me at the Slash Z.

Buddy and I

We had two horses when we lived at the Slash Z. Goldie was a high strung sorrel with a flax mane and tail. Only Sammy and Mary were allowed to ride him. The other horse was a big gentle bay named Buddy. I rode Buddy all the time.

One day I decided to become a trick rider. I practiced standing on Buddy's bare back and riding around the corral until that was no longer a challenge. Then I rode up the hill toward the house and the idea came to me to do a somersault on Buddy's back. I stopped Buddy, stood on his hips and did a somersault landing astraddle of him. I just needed a little more practice. So once again I stood up on Buddy's hips, took a deep breath and did another somersault. This time I missed the horse completely and landed on my back in front of Buddy. I took a hard blow to the back of my head and chipped one of my front teeth. As soon as I recovered my wind I let out a loud scream. Dad was down the hill milking the cow and he came running up to see how bad I was hurt.

Dad picked me up and carried me to the house. He cooked supper that night and sat me on a stool by the stove so he could keep an eye on me. I didn't have to set the table or clear it that night and neither did Mary. After supper Dad even did the dishes. The four of us kids went into the livingroom and sat around the fireplace. I was given Dad's big leather chair because I had been hurt. Before long I was out cold with my eyes wide open. This scared the other kids and they called Dad. He put all

71

of us in the car and headed to the only doctor in the area at Fort Huachuca.

I came to several hours later as Dad pulled the car back into the yard. It seems the doctor said I was to stay in bed the following day. Dad carried me to the house and I slept the rest of the night but when I woke up the next morning the other kids had gone to school and Dad had gone to work. No one woke me up and I was home alone.

Then I saw a big round Indian squaw sitting in the corner watching me. I guess Dad had made arrangements for her to stay with me and keep me in bed until he got home. She didn't speak any English. I was scared of her. I jumped out of bed, grabbed my clothes and escaped outside before she could catch me. I dressed and took a rope and went looking for Buddy. I found him and went riding until Dad and the kids came home that evening. I hadn't had anything to eat and I was hungry.

My trick riding days were over.

The Broom Closet

I t was my turn to do the supper dishes. There were some beans left on a plate and I was supposed to take any table scraps outside and give them to the dog. I was scared to go outside by myself after dark. I figured I could hide the plate of beans in the broom closet. Then in the morning I could feed them to the dog and Dad would never know.

Morning came and I had completely forgotten about the beans in the broom closet and there they stayed undetected. One day us kids got out Dad's box of family photos and while looking at them one of us accidently dropped a picture of Dad's father behind the kitchen counter. We told Dad about it when he came home and he felt really bad as it was the only photograph ever taken of his father. He wouldn't pull the counter loose from the wall to retrieve it. This wasn't his house and he didn't want to cause any damage. So the photo was lost.

Years later, after I was married, we went by the Slash Z. The house had been stripped of all the plumbing and was in a state of disrepair. Remembering the photo, we pulled the counter away from the wall and there unharmed was the photograph of Dad's father. Dad had died several years earlier so he never knew that the picture was finally back in the family.

As I walked through the house, I suddenly remembered the broom closet. I opened the door and sitting on the floor was a plate of dried up beans. I guess, It's safe to say we were probably the last people to live in that house.

Dad's father at an Abe Lincoln look-alike contest.

Uncle Bailey and our paternal grandmother.

PART FOUR

Dad Takes a Wife

Not long before we moved from the Slash Z Dad brought home a woman named Marion. She stayed with us. I don't know what the other kids thought but I thought she was temporary. When we moved to the Old Post Place in St. David she moved with us. Nothing changed by her living with us. We still had our freedom and spent most of our time outside and we still took care of ourselves. Then one day Dad called us kids together for a talk. This was serious. He asked us what we thought about him and Marion getting married. He was asking our permission.

The house at the Old Post Place was an old frame house typical for it's time with no indoor plumbing and no electricity. There was one room we didn't use. It had no windows and only an outside door that could be opened for light. We didn't use this door as it had no steps and there was a three foot drop to the ground. Like the rest of the house it had a rough wooden floor and the room was completely dark and empty.

It was into this room that we went to hold our discussion. We went in and closed the door and sat cross-legged on the rough floor in a circle, like little Indians. Sitting there in the dark each of us gave our opinion. Actually, I don't think any of us had paid too much attention to Marion. We liked her and certainly there was nothing negative. And so it was that we voted unanimously for this marriage. Then we returned to the kitchen and Mary gave Dad our verdict.

Suddenly it occurred to us - we had forgotten something. After they were married, should we call her Marion or would it be better if we called her Mom.

So back to the dark room we went, sat on the floor and once again we talked things over. We were very open and honest about how we felt when we had one of these meetings. We still loved and missed our mother very much and calling another woman Mom seemed almost disloyal. No one could take our mother's place in our lives or in our hearts. Nevertheless, all of us voted to call Marion , Mom. It was only fair to Marion. Then back to the kitchen once more to give Dad our new verdict.

One day, soon after our decision, when we came home from school Dad told us that he and Marion had driven to Lordsburg, New Mexico, and gotten married. He brought home a bunch of bananas as a special treat for us kids. I don't ever remember seeing or eating bananas again until I was grown.

Then there was another family meeting with Marion included. This took place around the kitchen table. Dad told Marion that us kids would continue to take care of ourselves and do chores, just as we had before she came. She was not a babysitter nor was she a workhorse. But there was something he did want her to do. I was nine and Mary was eleven. We needed a woman in our lives to teach us to be young ladies. Most of all he wanted us girls to have respectability.

So we continued to do the cooking, laundry and housekeeping and the boys did the outside chores. One thing to be said for Marion, she took care of herself. She kept her room clean and washed and ironed her own clothes and was in no way a burden.

Our lives took a definite turn for the better. We were all happier, especially Dad.

Marion

Marion was from New England. She was the eldest daughter of a prominent Boston banker. She could trace her family back to the Mayflower - a true blue blood. She had grown up in Boston's elite society. She was a lady.

At thirty eight Marion was attractive, slender and had a gray streak in the front of her dark natural curly hair. She loved hats. She always wore skirts and blouses. She put on white gloves when she went to town.

She didn't talk like we did. She had a distinctive Boston accent with broad a's and no r's. Her voice was soft and husky and she laughed a lot. We liked Marion.

Our step mother riding Badger -
the only Boquillas horse she ever rode.

Dad sitting on the steps at the Old Post Place.

Manners

We had already been taught cowboy etiquette with all our ma'ams and sirs, please and thank you's and even a few pardon me's and beg your pardons. When we came to the table we were washed, shirt tails tucked in and our hair combed. We asked for our food with, "Please pass...". We were mindful of the condition of our feet before entering the house.

Now we were going to learn about Emily Post. There was a clean white table cloth on the table and cloth napkins. The table was always set properly - fork on the left, knife and spoon on the right. No elbows or arms on the table - left hand in our lap and both feet flat on the floor. We always did this even if we were only eating beans and biscuits. The food was always brought to the table in bowls and serving dishes. Immediately after eating the table was cleared - including condiments, table cloth removed, dishes done and the kitchen cleaned. We ate in the dining room. No more eating in the kitchen.

Mom didn't eat with us. She took her meals alone and privately. This was one of her peculiarities. The only time she ate with us was at Thanksgiving and Christmas. However, she did come to the table and have coffee while the rest of us ate. She sat at the foot of the table and Dad at the head. Mary and I sat on one side and Sammy and Bailey on the other. Mealtimes were pleasant and happy.

The Nine O'Clock Sickness

The nine o'clock sickness was a mysterious illness from which you made a complete recovery at nine o'clock in the morning as soon as school started. Then you could go outside and play all day.

Well, Dad had a cure for this. If you said you were sick, you must be sick and the place for you was in bed even if at nine o'clock you felt much better. There was nothing worse than feeling good and having to stay in bed all day. Of course, if you really were sick you were glad to stay in bed.

Dad looked in on us once a day when we were sick, but it was Mary that took care of us. Sammy, Bailey and I would have an occasional bout with tonsilitis. If we had an earache Dad sat on the bed and blew warm cigarette smoke into our ear.

We were all very healthy. I remember having the nine o'clock sickness only once.

The Bonfire

In the summer we would hitch the mules to the wagon and go out to cut wood. The wood needed at least three months to season so we could use it for cooking and heating. We all worked at getting wood. The mesquite trees were cut down and the branches trimmed into long pieces of wood. These were loaded onto the wagon. When we had a good load we went home, unloaded the wagon and went back for more wood until we had enough to last us a year.

Mary always went with us to get wood. She was very strong and very good with an axe. Sammy and Bailey were also good wood cutters. I would be a good wood cutter too, when I got older and had a little more size to me. On these wood cutting trips, my job was to drag the brush that was trimmed off the wood and stack it in a clearing in a big pile.

We were very proud of this pile. We stacked it high and made sure the area around it was clear. Then after it had dried, we waited for a night with a full moon to set it on fire. It gave off so much light and heat that the red ants thought it was daytime and came out of their dens.

We had one of these bonfires while we were at the Old Post Place. We never gave it a thought that the fire could be seen from a great distance. We had never lived this close to other people. The fire was easily visible from St. David. We were really enjoying our bonfire when here came the Mormans.

They thought our house was on fire and they came to help us put it out.

We had been warned that it could be difficult living close to the Mormons but they treated us like their own. After dark on Valentine's Day there was a knock on the door. When we went to the door no one was there, but on the porch was a big sack of cookies. These people were good neighbors.

After Dark

One summer day during the rainy season I wanted to walk to my friend's house. Dad gave me permission to go but I had to be home before dark. No problem. It was only a mile.

I was having so much fun I didn't notice the sun go down. Suddenly I realized it was getting dark so I hurriedly departed. Even though it was late I stayed on the road - no short cut through the mesquites.

Well, it was dark long before I got home and there I was all alone and afraid of the dark. As I got closer to home I could hear the hounds, Mac and Spike, barking. I knew I would feel a lot better if they would come and walk me the rest of the way home. I began calling them but not very loud as I didn't want anything or anybody to hear me except the dogs.

When I didn't come home Dad became worried about me and sent Sammy out to find me. Time passed and Dad decided to look for both of us.

As Sammy came to a bend in the road he could hear me calling, "Here, Mac. Here, Spike." He hid and waited for me. Just as I came around the bend Sammy jumped out at me with his arms raised above his head and yelled as loud as he could. At that exact moment lightning struck close by and lit up the world as bright as day and there was a deafening clap of thunder. All I saw was a silhouette of a creature that looked ten feet tall with upraised arms coming to get me. I clasped both hands together under my chin and prepared to meet my doom. My knees turned to jelly and hit the dirt road. I fell over backwards. The last thing I remember was screaming. Then I fainted. The next thing I knew there were car lights very close and Dad and Sammy were trying to revive me.

Sammy was in big trouble. He never outgrew his love of scaring someone.

The War Hoop

We could all yell loud if the occasion arose. It was a Foster thing. But Dad could really yell. He had this particular yell we called the war hoop. We were allowed a lot of freedom. We just had to stay within earshot of the house if Dad was home. We knew we could go pretty far and still hear Dad but the exact distance really never crossed our minds - until one day.

We were living at the Old Post Place about a mile from St. David. We had never lived this close to other people before. So we went out to play and we were mindful to keep within earshot of the house. We heard Dad's war hoop and started for home. Imagine our surprise when we got there and found half the people in St. David had come to the rescue. They had heard Dad's war hoop too. To us kids it had almost a musical quality to it, but to the Mormons it was bloodcurdling. No telling what must have gone through their minds. But one thing for sure, Dad's war hoop could be heard for at least a mile.

Dad took pride in his voice and liked to show its effect on Mom. When he was on his way home on horseback but still quite a distance from the house, he would give a war hoop. Shortly thereafter, a puff of smoke would rise from the chimney and could be seen over the tops of the mesquites. Mom had heard his war hoop. She had stoked the fire in the wood stove and put the beans on to boil.

PART FIVE

The Company

The Company was a good outfit to work for especially for a family man. He was furnished with a house, utilities and groceries. The pay wasn't as much as it was other places but room and board were furnished. Other outfits may pay more but the housing wasn't as good and you bought your own groceries.

The Company had good housing - all with running water and indoor plumbing. All the houses were good houses and kept in good repair. The utilities were a fifty five gallon drum of kerosene and all the wood you could chop - a mesquite thicket.

Groceries were what was in the commissary and it was well stocked. There was no mayonnaise but there was everything it took to make it so we made our own. This was true of other things as well. So with a little work and imagination you could make almost anything. You turned in your grocery list on pay day and groceries were delivered once a month. Groceries were groceries. If you ordered a lot or a little it didn't affect your pay check.

Without refrigeration, butchering was only done in the winter. We hung the meat up on the north porch to chill at night and wrapped it in a heavy "meat tarp" in the morning and laid it on the cold cement floor. The sun never shined in the winter time on the north porch. Taking care of the meat was just one of the chores. At mealtime the cook unwrapped the meat and cut steaks and then wrapped the meat back in the tarp. You never cut off more than was going to be cooked . Leaving the meat in large chunks helped it to keep. We never had any meat spoil.

Dad was a good meat cutter and he taught all of us kids how to cut meat. We had a heavy meat board to cut on and sharp knives and a meat saw.

Every camp was brought a side of bacon with the rind on it every month. The bacon was dry cured and kept without refrigeration even in the summer. Cutting bacon was part of preparing breakfast. You only cut as much as you were going to cook. The rind was used to flavor the beans.

In the summer the Company brought each camp a large ham every month and canned salmon. Also in the summer they brought us a large wheel of Longhorn cheese, cabbage and carrots.

Each camp had two dairy cows that the Company provided feed for and they provided feed for chickens but you supplied your own chickens. Seeds for a vegetable garden were provided if you wanted to plant a garden. You even had a team of mules and a plow available to use.

About the only things the Company didn't provide were personal items like toothpaste, shampoo and deodorant. We never let any food spoil and we never wasted anything. This was an unwritten law.

A cowboy rode Company horses but he supplied his own horse gear and bedroll.

The Commissary

This is a list of the things we could order from the commissary. Groceries were delivered once a month. This was part of the cowboy's wages along with the house he lived in. The cost of food and supplies were not deducted from his wages.

Coffee

Tea

Cocoa

Flour

Cornmeal

Salt

Pepper

Yeast

Baking Powder

Baking Soda

Spices

Cornstarch

Lima Beans

Navy Beans

Black Eyed Peas

Coconut

Sugar

Brown Sugar

Powered Sugar

Tapioca

Jello

Jello Puddings

Plain Gelatin

Wesson Oil

Crisco Shortening

Lard

Pinto Beans

Catsup

Pickles

Vinegar

Rice	Louisiana Hot Sauce
Macaroni	Chili Powder
Potatoes	Canned Green Chili
Onions	Tomato Sauce
Garlic	Canned Tomatoes
Dried Apples	Canned Corn
Dried Peaches	Canned Cream Style Corn
Dried Apricots	Canned Peas
Prunes	Canned Green Beans
Raisins	Canned Hominy
Quaker Oatmeal	Canned Beets
Cream of Wheat	Carnation Canned Milk
Corn Flakes	Canned Salmon
Saltine Crackers	Gallon Can of Cherry Preserves
Graham Crackers	Log Cabin Syrup
Five Gallon Can of Honey	Clorox
Spic and Span	White King Laundry Detergent
Chore Girl	Fels Naptha Bar Soap
Johnson's Window Wax	Palmolive Hand Soap
Toilet Paper	Lava Hand Soap
Old English Furniture Polish	Life Bouy Hand Soap
Dust Mop	Ivory Hand Soap
Mop	Vel Dish Detergent
Broom	Dutch Cleanser

SUMMER: Carrots, Cabbage, Longhorn Cheese, Large Ham,
Side of Bacon

WINTER: Butchered Beef and Pork, Side of Bacon
Utilities: 55 gallon drum of kerosene
Vegetable seeds (if you wanted to plant a garden)
Morton Curing Salt (if you wanted to cure fresh pork)

FEED: Cotton Seed Cake Pellets - Milk Cow Range Cows
       Whole Oats - Horses Pig
       Milo Maize - Chickens (you provided the chickens)
       Alfalfa Hay - Milk Cow Milk Pen Calf

The Cowboy

To me the cowboy was a wonderful person. His movements were sure and purposeful. He always wore boots and his walk was slightly bowlegged. I'm sure he could walk long distances if needed but he really preferred to ride.

He smoked Bull Durham and could roll a cigarette and light it in almost any condition - rain, wind, dark or while sitting on a snakey horse that wouldn't stand still.

He was very much at home on the back of a horse and could put in long hours in the saddle. He was burned dark by the sun and he had wrinkles from squinting. He was good natured and had a great sense of humor. He would tell or listen to the same stories over and over and they just got better with time.

He didn't have much but he was generous with both time and possessions.

Cowboys weren't comfortable standing. They would squat - one knee up and one knee down. They could squat like this for a long time occasionally shifting their weight by alternating which knee was up and which knee was down.

He carried wooden kitchen matches in his shirt pocket. These he struck on his leg by raising his knee and pulling his Levis tight. One quick motion and the match was lit. Of course, he could always light a match by flicking the head of it off with his thumb nail.

The first thing a cowboy did when he came in the house

was remove his hat. That was good manners. His hat left a permanent mark on his hair and his brow was white from no sun. He was clean shaven - maybe a mustache - and he kept his hair short.

Cowboys were kind and considerate to women. They never swore or told off color stories in the presence of a woman. But they expected something in return. They wanted their women to be lady-like. - no drinking, swearing, smoking, gambling and no coarse language.

A cowboy was honest and his word was his bond. A firm hand shake was a contract.

It was among these good men that we grew up.

The Wolf Place

In 1947 we moved from the Old Post Place in St. David to the Wolf Place. At the time it was a two-man camp, a married man and a single man. Johnny Pitts was the single man and he stayed in the small room on the back porch and took his meals with the family. He kept a five gallon can of honey mixed with prunes in his room. Seems he had a sweet tooth.

Shortly after we moved, the Company issued each of the boys four horses and they began riding with Dad. They didn't draw any pay but they were good help. Then Johnny Pitts was moved to another camp and our family lived alone at the Wolf Place.

The Wolf Place had a nice two bedroom house with hardwood floors, indoor plumbing, a large kitchen, a large living room and north and south screened-in porches with cement floors. On the south porch there was a small room originally intended for use as a pantry. There were five of these houses on the Company. One at the Horse Camp in the Dragoon Mountains, one at the Whetstone Camp in the Whetstone Mountains, one at the Wolf Place and two at the Headquarters near Fairbank. These were probably built in the 1930's. The Stone House Camp near St. David was just a common old frame house as was the house at the Old Post Place between St. David and the Horse Camp. At the Hereford Camp there was a huge unfinished mansion started by the Moson family.

There was also a frame house in Fairbank for the windmiller and his family.

One of the first things Dad built was a cooler on the back porch just right of the outside door. It was the size of a section of screen and about two feet deep and extended outside. This was a frame covered with gunny sacks. A large dishpan was turned upside down on top to deflect the water and a hose was left dripping on it. It had a shelf and cupboard door. This kept the milk and butter cool. We used it like a refrigerator. It was cool enough to make jello.

Next Dad built a pig pen down in the big grove of willow trees east of the house. After that he built a cow pen and stall. There was already a good sized horse corral. Later he built another corral with a loading chute.

There was a chicken house and chicken pen under the big tree. These Dad tore down as the chicken house was full of blue bugs and he didn't want them to get on his chickens. There was also an outhouse next to the chicken house for the cowboys to use during roundup, but it needed to be cleaned out and rather than do this Dad tore it down too. After that the cowboys used Mother Nature's facilities.

The last person to use the outhouse was the flunky, even though he had been asked not to. He never noticed the big rattlesnake that was napping in there. When the flunky came out, the snake followed him and was killed by the cowboys.

Mom liked water lilies so Dad built her a nice lily pond out of weathered limestone rocks. We hauled the rocks in from the top of the hills north of the house in the mule wagon. Mom and Mary put the ends of their colored embroidery thread on the rocks and the orioles used them in their nests in the big cottonwood tree. They also fed the birds at the pond.

Dad's next big project was the bunkhouse under the big tree. There was no practical use for this house but Dad wanted to build a house reminiscent of his log cabin in Patagonia.

When the crossties were replaced on the railroad the old used crossties were stacked to the side and burned. The section foreman at Lewis Springs told Dad he had a pile of used crossties if he wanted them.

Dad and I made trip after trip with the mule wagon until we had hauled all the crossties home. It didn't take long to build what was then called the bunkhouse. It had a heavy wood door, one window with shutters, a dirt floor and a pole in the middle to support the roof. The roof was a layer of crossties with at least a foot of soil on top. The space between the crossties was chinked with mud but Dad didn't like the black soil we had on the river. Instead he wanted the red soil from Fry as it more closely resembled the color of the soil in Patagonia. To get the red soil he wanted, Dad put a wash tub in the trunk of the car and every time he went to Fry for the mail, he brought home a tubful of red dirt.

Going to Fry was no easy task. The car never started on its own. A horse had to be caught and saddled. Then Dad tied onto the front bumper with his rope and pulled the car until it started. It was Mom's job to get the car running and keep it running until Dad unsadddled his horse and took over the job of driving. This ritual was just part of going to town.

Dad and I were proud of the bunkhouse on completion. Dad even put a small wood stove in it.

Snake Flat and the River

One of the first things we did when we moved to a new place was to explore. Sammy and Bailey came home and told Mary and I they had found a place where we could swim. It was up at Snake Flat. There was a large galvanized trough with artesian water flowing through it. This sounded good especially to me as I knew it couldn't be too deep.

So the next morning we all put our swim suits on under our clothes and started out. Snake Flat was several miles from the house but that was hardly any distance to us.

We came to the trough and it was all the boys said it was. We peeled off our clothes down to our swim suits and into the water we went. We splashed and played and had lots of fun. Then it was time to go home. We started to put our clothes on over our wet suits when one of us noticed a leech on our skin. On closer examination there were lots of leeches on all of us. We pulled off all the leeches we could reach on ourselves and Mary looked us over and got the ones we missed or couldn't reach. This was our first encounter with leeches and we didn't go back there to swim again.

Then Sammy and Bailey came home with another story of a swimming hole in the river. This one was deep and only about a half mile from the house. The floods had washed out a good sized hole next to the bank under a willow tree. It was a clean open hole with only a few roots next to the bank. The ground sloped down on three sides with a straight drop under the tree. It couldn't have been more perfect.

There were some good sized suckers in there so it served as a fishing hole too. We ate the suckers even if they were boney. We didn't take them home. We cooked and ate them on the river bank. We thought they were pretty good even if the grown-ups didn't think they were fit to eat. They were better than the fish we had been eating.

In those days the river was wide and had lots of water in it. The summer rains overflowed stock tanks and ponds and brought perch and goldfish to the river. We had a window screen wired onto two yucca poles that we used to catch fish with. None of these fish were very big. We threw the goldfish back and kept the perch and minnows. We cleaned the perch but the minnows were too small to clean - there wouldn't be anything left - so we cooked them whole. We poked a hole in the minnows before they went into the rusty frying pan because if we didn't they exploded. Sometimes Sammy and Bailey would drink lots of water and swallow a few minnows so they could feel them swimming in their stomachs. Mary and I never did this.

Mr. Hansen had a hive of bees on the east side of the horse pasture fence. Sammy and Bailey smoked and robbed these bees for some fresh comb honey to eat with our fish and watercress which grew along the river. There was plenty to eat at home, but we hadn't quite out grown foraging for whatever we could find.

Mr. Hansen bladed the dirt road between Fry and Bisbee. When he robbed his bees he always stopped by the house with a dishpan full of comb honey for us. I think it was this act of generosity that shamed us into leaving his bees alone. However, there were wild bees that Sammy and Bailey robbed. They were good at it and didn't get stung.

I didn't go in the deep part of the swimming hole as I was still afraid of the water. I never learned to swim and neither did Bailey but this didn't stop him from having fun. He would hold his breath and walk into the water until he went out of sight and then come walking out on the other side.

After every big flood we went down to the river to check on the swimming hole and it was always there. Then one summer the floods did fill up the swimming hole but the other kids had already left home.

Plaza and Other Trees

When we moved back to the Wolf Place we were enthralled by the huge cottonwood tree near the house. It was huge and beautifully shaped. Mom immediately named it Plaza and from that time on it was referred to by name. It was only fitting that a tree of this stature should have a name.

We didn't recognize this tree. Years before we had lived at the Wolf Place and this tree was only a small cottonwood. It had grown into one of the biggest cottonwood trees on the river.

One of the first things Dad did when we moved back was to put all of us kids on horseback and take us up to Snake Flat where there was a large grove of cottonwood trees. There on the ground was a tree even larger than Plaza. It had been struck by lightning and was laid out in all directions like the spokes of a wagon wheel. He wanted us to see this tree while it was still intact before time and nature obscured it.

Lightning had struck one of several large cottonwood trees just in front of the house and the charred remains were still there when we moved back to the Wolf Place.

There was another grove of cottonwoods south of the house on the sacaton flat. Also there was a large grove of willow trees and one cottonwood between the house and the river. This was truly a beautiful camp.

Dad built a sturdy tree house in Plaza out of two by eight inch planks. The first room was just a floor with a bench on two sides and the tree formed the other two walls. Then you could go through a fork in the tree to another floor but Dad ran out of materials so this floor was only about two feet wide. There was a ladder in front of the tree that went up through the floor of the tree house. It was a wonderful place to sit.

I think Dad loved cottonwoods as he took the mule wagon down to the river in February one year and cut four large cottonwood limbs and brought them home. He planted these in the yard. He named the limbs for each of us kids. They were positioned to the four corners of the world - east, west, north and south. We watered and tended the trees faithfully. Each of us examined our tree every day looking for the first leaves to appear. Cottonwoods are easy to propagate and we were so sure our tree would grow and thrive. But strangely, only Bailey's tree leafed out. Dad figured he must have planted the other limbs upside down so he took the dead limbs out and left "Bailey" to grow alone. This tree is now a big tree at the corner of the yard.

A couple of years later Dad took the snubbing post out of the center of the horse corral and in its place he planted another cottonwood limb. This time he marked the end to be left up. This tree was planted in 1952. Whoever came in from riding first carried buckets of water from the horse trough and watered the tree. The purpose of this tree was to provide shade for any horse left in the corral. This tree is still standing today.

Between the house and Snake Flat there was a large stand of young cottonwood trees growing close together on the west side of the river down inside of the river bank. All the cranes from up and down the river nested in this stand of trees. This was known as Crane Town. Mesquite thickets ringed the sacaton flats along the river. In later years this part of Boquillas was leased out and farmed. Most of the trees were taken out - mesquites, cottonwoods and willows - and sugar beets were grown along the river for one year.

I think the big cottonwood tree we called Plaza is dying. I believe it got a lot of water from the septic tank and with no one living in the house there is no water for the tree.

Dad after he planted the Cottonwood tree in the horse corral.

Indians and Fossils

When we first moved back to the Wolf Place in 1947, there were abundant pottery shards on any open ground especially around the house and horse pasture. One day on the way home from school Sammy didn't stay on the road like the rest of us but walked about ten feet to the side. There he spotted two small clay pots turned upside down and half buried. Later just above the horse pasture he found another bowl partially buried. This one was made of porous lava rock with three legs on the bottom. Inside was a tomahawk. Arrowheads and beads could also be found lying on top of the ground.

When Sammy and Bailey were riding and they saw an arrowhead, they got off of their horse and picked it up. Then they stuck it in the next fence post or gate post they came to. It wasn't unusual to see a half dozed arrowheads in almost any gate post. One day Sammy brought home a beautiful little flat white bead. It was a perfect five pointed star with a hole in the middle. This one he gave to me. These artifacts were plentiful and common. No value and not much attention was given them. Usually they were given to the first person that came by that showed any interest in them.

We had heavy summer rains and in a year or two most of it had washed away. The same was true of the mastodons. Sammy came home one day with a story of a large bone - it was larger than anything he had ever seen. Dad was sure it was nothing more than perhaps the shoulder blade of a bull. But when he and

Sammy rode back for another look, Dad knew what it was. It was the tusk of a mastodon lying in a shallow gully northwest of the house. Dad notified the University of Arizona but they weren't interested. At that time it was believed the mastodons were gone before early man came to this area.

Not long afterward, Sammy found another mastodon at the head of Horse Thief Springs. This one appeared to be mostly intact. There was also another animal at the site - not far from the mastodon. To us it looked like some sort of reptile. There were lots of pieces of what appeared to be armor. The edges were irregular as if broken and about three inches in diameter. There was a pattern on one side and the other side was porous like bone. It closely resembled the skin of a horned toad only in a larger pattern. There was enough to have easily filled a large wash tub lying on top of the ground. Also there were "fins" about the size of two men's hands put together. All this was in the same area but separate from the mastodon.

Again Dad notified the University of Arizona and still no interest. A couple of years later a neighbor, Louie Escapule, found a couple of spear heads in the mastodon. Then the University of Arizona was interested and excavated the site. By the time Louie and the archeologists came to the site the rains had washed the second animal away. They theorized that what we described to them was scale from the teeth of the mastodon. Unfortunately we hadn't saved any pieces to show them.

While on a school picnic at Charleston in 1952, I found about a six foot long row of these "fins" sticking out of the gravel in the river bottom. They didn't look like teeth to me. This time we didn't contact the University of Arizona.

Summer

We had a lot more rain in the forties and fifties than we do now. During the first part of the fifties during the rainy season our only way out was on horseback. A detour was made around the mud holes and soon the detour became a mud hole too so then a detour was made on the other side. When this became a mud hole the road was impassable. This was especially the case for the road that paralleled the river. We really didn't care about the roads as we didn't need to get out.

The river was wide and the floods big. After a big rain we would step outside and listen. We could tell by the roar of the river how big the flood was. If the river was really roaring everybody including Mom walked down to the river to have a look. The river could be truly awesome.

It took days for the river to go down enough to cross on horseback. After a big flood all the water gaps - wire fences across the river and sand washes - were washed out. This meant building fence - not a cowboy's favorite job - but it had to be done. The outside boundary fences were especially important. The neighbors let the Boquillas cowboy repair the fence they both shared. There was one exception. Frank Crane came by in his jeep and picked up Dad and they both put the water gaps back in that bordered Frank's place.

I think it was in the spring of 1949, that the river dried up at the Wolf Place. The cattle watered out of the river so this left them without water. Dad harnessed up the mules and hooked onto the fresno - a large scoop - and dug for water at intervals so the cows could get water without walking too far. This had to be done every couple of days as the cows caved in the holes and they had to be dug out again. The rains were especially welcome that summer.

As long as we lived at the Wolf Place that was the only time this happened.

Rattlesnakes

There were sink holes on the flat below the house and these made excellent breeding places for rattlesnakes and a good place to spend the winter. When we returned to the Wolf Place, there was definitely a rattlesnake problem.

That first summer Dad and the boys killed twenty three rattlers in the horse trap alone. The horse trap was a small pasture used for the milk pen calf and a place to put a horse overnight to be used to wrangle horses on in the morning. Of course, there were lots of snakes around the house and the horse pasture.

A snake bit one of the horses on the nose and he swelled up and had trouble breathing. Dad cut the sharp spikes off of a yucca plant and as gently as possible tapped the horse on the nose with a handful of these sharp spikes making numerous punctures for the venom and fluid to drain and give the horse relief. The horse lived.

Most cowboys were good at doctoring and taking care of the livestock. This was part of their job. Dad was exceptionally good at this and he extended his doctoring skills to us kids but Mom would have no part of this. She wanted a real doctor. However, she did allow Dad to care for her little dog, Bonnie Wee, when she was bitten by a rattlesnake in the yard. The snake bit her on the side of the face and Dad said, because of the location of the bite, she would recover. And she did.

Whenever a rattlesnake was killed his head was cut off and buried as a safety precaution while his rattles were being cut off.

113

The rattles were brought to the house. This way we could keep count of how many snakes were killed and their approximate size and age.

The game chickens were helpful in reducing the rattlesnake population. When they found a snake they formed a circle around it and sounded the alarm. Then Dad or the boys would kill the snake with a pitchfork. If no one came to the aid of the chickens they would kill the snake themselves. There were lots of big snakes on the river. Dad killed one snake that the chickens had and it was longer than the pitchfork.

One day Sammy and Bailey were walking along the railroad tracks when they saw a big rattlesnake. They decided to kill it with rocks but the snake had other ideas and tried to make an escape in the loose rocks on the embankment. As the snake was disappearing into the rocks one boy caught him by the tail and held on while the other cut off his rattles with a sharp stick. They didn't have a pocket knife. They were young - only nine and ten - and hadn't yet learned to twist the rattles off. Well, this was an unhappy snake. He reappeared by the end of his tail and went between the boys. All parties concerned were moving fast and the snake escaped with his life but not with his rattles. About a year later the boys were riding above Snake Flat when they spotted a large rattlesnake in the bottom of a deep sink hole. They didn't want to ride on by. They wanted to kill this snake and add his rattles to the collection at home.

Sammy found a long yucca pole and held the snake's head down while Bailey got off of his horse and took down his rope. He opened up the horn knot an the end of the rope making a loop. Then he jumped down into the hole with the snake and put the loop over the snake's tail. Then he climbed out and jerked the snake out of the hole onto flat ground. The boys killed him and brought his rattles home.

Winter

Our winters were colder and wetter than they are now. During the winter months there was a thick layer of ice on the watering troughs that had to be broken so the livestock could drink. Usually the horses broke the ice on the trough in the horse pasture but there was no way the milk cow or her calf could break the ice on the trough in the corral. This was where most of the chickens watered too. So whoever milked the cow in the morning took an axe and chopped the ice out of the troughs. It was about four to six inches thick.

We also had more snow in the winter. I remember one especially cold morning when all the windows in the house were covered with ice crystals and looked like giant snow flakes. We didn't keep a fire going at night so the house got pretty cold. We were all good fire builders so it didn't take us long to warm up the house. We didn't heat the bedrooms. Milking the cow at five in the morning was a pretty cold chore. The ground was usually frozen. The cow was like a furnace. At first it was like milking icicles until the milk warmed things up. While we milked we would snuggle up close to the cow and get warm.

We fed the horses grain in the winter. We hung the gunny sack morals on the horses and they ate while we milked. When the milking was done the horses had finished eating. We pulled off their gunny sack morals, picked up the milk and headed back to a warm house. There is nothing like coming in from the cold to a warm house and wood fire.

Then it was time to cook breakfast, pack lunches, clean the kitchen and go to school.

The Christmas Tree

Bailey and I were nine when we moved back to the Wolf Place and the youngest in the family. With Christmas approaching, Dad called us kids together and told us we were getting too old for a Christmas tree. Then he asked for our opinion. Of course, we all agreed with him so he didn't buy a tree when he went to Fry.

That night while the four of us kids were sitting around the table in the living room and Dad and Mom were in their room, we discussed the matter of the Christmas tree. None of us were ready for Christmas without a tree.

The boys said they knew where a lone cedar tree was growing about a quarter of a mile from the house up on the black brush hills. This was the only cedar tree in the area. So it was decided that Sammy and Bailey would chop it down and carry it home. Mary and I would slip out of the house and bring in the big box of decorations from the garage. It was moonlight so none of us needed a lantern.

When the boys returned with the cedar tree, Mary and I had the decorations ready. The boys made a stand for the tree and we all decorated it. Then we went to bed pleased that we hadn't been discovered.

When Dad got up the next morning and saw the tree, he was truly surprised. He felt so bad for not getting us a tree. We didn't want him to feel bad but we were proud of our accomplishment. After that Dad always brought home a Christmas tree.

Sammy's Ride for Help

It was our first winter back at the Wolf Place and it was cold. There was lots of snow that year.

One day there was a very heavy snow storm and before long there was about a foot of snow on the ground and it was still snowing hard. Mom began having chest pains. She needed a doctor. The car wouldn't start and I don't think it would have made it over the road anyway.

Us kids were so scared. We thought she was going to die. I think Dad thought so too. He was very worried. The only hope was the Escapules. They lived about five miles down the river and they had a three quarter ton Studebaker truck.

Dad needed to stay with Mom so he put Sammy on the biggest, fastest horse he had - a big brown horse named Beaver. I watched as Sammy rode Beaver at a fast lope down the road and was soon lost from sight in the snow.

He got to the Escapules and stopped in the front yard. He was half frozen and packed with snow. He had almost run the horse to death. The men pulled Sammy off the horse and carried him into the house where they turned him over to the women to be cared for. They put him by the wood fire and hung his jacket up to dry.

The Escapules got in the pickup and drove through the snow to our house. They put Mom and Dad in the truck and all four of them headed for Tombstone and a doctor.

After Sammy had been warmed by the fire and Beaver had caught his wind, he rode back home through the snow. He unsaddled his horse and came in to get warm again.

119

Just before dark the Escapules brought Mom and Dad back home. Mom was alright. It was wonderful to have good neighbors. That was the only time we had to ask for help.

Sammy was only ten years old.

The Yoke

We had a milk pen calf that sucked through the fence and at milking time there was no milk. Of course, the cow had to cooperate with the calf and stand next to the fence.

Since Bailey was the woodcutter, the job of making a yoke fell to him. He took an axe and crawled through the fence into the horse trap. He was looking for a green mesquite tree with a "y" shaped limb. This would be cut and fitted on the calf's neck preventing him from putting his head far enough through the fence to reach the cow. After a hard swing, the axe glanced off the tree and struck Bailey in the end of his foot - splitting his shoe and foot.

I was in the house when I heard Bailey. He was softly singing a slow, terrible song, "Ooh - ooh - ooh". I saw him come to the fence, crawl through and continue on to the house. All the while softly singing, "Ooh - ooh - ooh", and hoping on one foot.

There was lots of blood. Dad removed his shoe and Mom cut his sock off. Then Dad wrapped Bailey's foot in a clean flour sack, carried him into the living room and laid him on his back on the day bed we used as a couch. His foot was propped high on pillows. All the while, Bailey never quit singing his song. I begged Dad to take him to the doctor but he was firm and stern. He said Bailey would be alright and he was. He was just nine years old. I still feel bad when I remember this.

The Explosion

We started the fires in the wood stoves with kerosene. First we opened all the dampers, filled the fire-box about half full with wood chips and then added as much wood as would fit into the stove. Over this we poured about a cup of kerosene. All the lids except one were put back on. Then we lit a match and threw it in and put the last lid on. And the fire roared. When Dad built the fire he poured in a lot of kerosene and the fire really roared. It was scary.

The kerosene we had then was much different than it is now. It was flammable! Today's kerosene is slow to light and it certainly won't roar. At least not for me.

We came home from school one day and it was my turn to build a fire. Dad and Mom had gone to Fry to get the mail and hadn't returned yet. I took the lids off the stove and there were a few coals left over from the last fire but not enough to start a new one. I knew better than to use kerosene when there were coals in the stove so I cleaned out the stove very thoroughly - ashes - everything. Then I built a fire. I didn't realize a hot stove was the same thing as a hot coal.

I poured in the kerosene and replaced the lids, all but one. When I started to strike the match I saw a little plume of smoke. I knew that was a bad sign but I didn't know how bad. I struck the match, stood back as far as possible, turned my head and threw in the match. What an explosion! It blew all the lids off the stove and blew the chimney off. I was singed. I lost my eyelashes, my eyebrows, the fuzz on my arms and some of the hair on my head.

But at least I didn't catch on fire. This was my first explosion. I was nine years old.

Mary and Sammy

Everyone loved Mary and Sammy. They were the golden children in the family. They were clearly our parents' favorites. I don't think Bailey and I minded as we loved them too. They were blonde and blue eyed with outgoing personalities. They had charisma. Bailey and I had hazel eyes and dark dish-water blonde hair. And we were shy. We both had dimples like Dad and Bailey had very long thick eyelashes. But Bailey and I had something special going for us - we were twins. We had each other.

As I grew up my stepmother would often ask, "Why can't you be more like Mary?" And in my ignorant wisdom I would reply, "Because I am me." But in my heart I really did want to be like Mary. She was everything I wasn't. I knew no matter how hard I tried I would never be like Mary so I settled in to be me.

Growing up

The day came when Mary no longer wanted to be outside with us. She wanted to be in the house with Mom. They formed a close bond. There was so much Mary wanted to learn. I didn't fit in and I felt like I was in the way. I had spent too much time outside and I couldn't give it up. The only time I spent in the house was when I had to.

The Company had sent the extra man to another camp and given the boys each a string of four horses. They helped Dad and did the work normally done by the extra man but they were only nine and ten and drew no pay.

I didn't fit in there either but Dad and the boys were more tolerant. There was always a horse for me to ride but it was understood that for me the house came first. If the dishes weren't done by the time Dad had his cup of coffee after breakfast he wouldn't wait for me. No horse was left in the corral and there would be no riding out and catching up. I learned to be fast. I wasn't left behind very often. If I wanted to go I had to pull my own weight as much as possible. This meant wrestling calves. It was important that the boys learned to rope so I flanked calves. There were always calves with screw worms in their navels or where their brands were peeling. These calves weren't very big but I managed to get kicked and trampled a lot.

I wanted to learn to rope but Dad was very firmly against this. The boys were not to let me use their ropes ever. The only thing in the way of a rope I carried on my saddle was a piggin' string.

This was for hobbling my horse or for use as a quirt. Dad was so sure if I had a rope I would manage to cut off my fingers and no one would marry me.

It wasn't long until the boys were good hands. I had one foot in each world. I knew the time would come when I would have to go inside - and I did - but it would be a while.

Sammy at age 11 - already a good hand.

Me holding Mom's little dog, Bonnie Wee at the Wolf Place.

Me below the house at Wolf Place.

Dad driving Pete and Molly over to be hooked up to the wagon. Off to the right is Bonnie Wee. She always went with the mules.

Mary, Bailey, Betty and Sammy.

The Snake Skin

Sammy and Bailey were always killing and skinning snakes, usually rattlesnakes, for hat bands. One day I skinned a beautiful red racer. Just how it got dead I don't remember. I would like to think one of the boys killed it but since it was my snake, I must have done the deed. Anyway it had a beautiful skin.

I was going to cover my belt with it. I didn't want to put salt on it like the boys did with their skins because the salt made the skins stiff. So I rolled it up and hid it under the bed that I shared with Mary until I could figure out what to do with it so it would stay soft.

Time passed and other things took my attention. Then one day Mary said something smelled really bad in our room and she started hunting for the cause. Before long she discovered my beautiful and now foul smelling snake skin. She ordered me to get rid of it. It was so pretty I just couldn't part with it. I washed it good with soap and water and put a generous amount of Mary's perfume on it. Then I rolled it up again and back under the bed it went. This time the smell was truly awful and Mary saw to it that I really did get rid of it. This broke my heart. So much for having a beautiful snake skin belt.

The Red Soled Shoes

Some kind and generous person gave Dad a pair of low cut brown leather shoes for one of the boys. They were almost new and expensive. They had thick light red soles like tire treads. I thought they were nice looking shoes.

Dad called the boys over and had them take off their tennis shoes. He was going to see which boy these fine shoes would fit. First it was Sammy's turn but his feet were too big. Next came Bailey but his feet were too big too.

I was standing there watching all this when Dad turned to me and told me to take off my shoes. At first I didn't understand. These were boys shoes. Girls didn't wear boys shoes and boys didn't wear girls shoes. He tried the shoes on my feet and they were a perfect fit. This was like the Cinderella story with a bad twist.

These shoes no longer looked nice to me. Certainly they were better than the shoes I'd been wearing and they were comfortable. But they were boys shoes and I hated them. My dignity was hurt.

Every time I went outside I saw my tracks. They looked like tire tracks. I couldn't get away from these tracks - they were everywhere - and they were a reminder of my boys shoes. Even when I was riding I couldn't get away from these tracks. There they were when I came to a gate. I didn't know I had been so many places. There was no place I could go that I hadn't already been.

Finally I outgrew these shoes and they still looked like new and were passed on to someone else.

Dumb Dog

Some cowboy had given us a big clumsy red pup. He was exceptionally large and dumb and he had a deformed hind leg. He ran around chewing on everything, wouldn't mind and was just a general nuisance. But Dad had hopes he would turn into a fine dog one day

It so happened Dad was at the woodpile one day and so was the pup. The pup was stumbling around chewing on everything he came to. He stepped over the wagon tongue and stopped, staring off into space with his tail across the tongue of the wagon. Dad liked bob-tailed animals - especially dogs. He picked up the axe and with a quick chop the pup lost his tail. He jumped and looked around not quite sure what had happened. He didn't even yelp. He saw his tail lying there on the ground, picked it up and began chewing on it. This so disgusted Dad that he loaded the pup in the car and gave him back to the cowboy.

The Pig's Head

One of my chores was feeding the pig. The pig pen was below the house in the big grove of willow trees. These pigs the Company brought to us to be fattened up were wild and mean. This one was no exception. When I crawled up on the fence so I could pour his bucket of soaked grain and milk into the trough he would charge me hitting the fence. I held on tight so I didn't land on my back with slop all over me. I knew he couldn't get over the fence but still it worried me. If some poor chicken got into the pen to share his food he was caught and eaten. This particular pig had already eaten a couple of chickens and he had a wicked look to him.

I was glad when Dad got the barrel of water heated and it was time to butcher the pig. After he was killed he would be slid into a barrel of hot lye water and taken out and scraped. More dirt than hair came off and he was clean as a whistle. His head was cut off behind his ears and he was drawn and ready to be cut up. I never watched when Dad killed an animal but I did watch the butchering. Once the animal was dead it lost it's identity so it didn't bother me.

The Company provided Morton curing salt for sausage, bacon and ham. Dad made good sausage and bacon but he didn't make hams. We ate these as pork. Butchering was always done in the winter as there was no refrigeration. We took half of the pig to the Hereford Camp. Then they butchered the next pig and gave us half.

The boys had the job of cleaning up where the pig had been

butchered. We didn't eat the feet or the head. These were thrown away.

About dark I decided to go down to the willow grove and look at the empty pig pen. It would be quiet and peaceful there without the pig. There was a trail from the house down to the willow grove. It wound through the sacaton clumps. I was small so the sacaton came up past my waist. I was walking along thinking of nothing in particular with my head down looking at the trail.

As I was almost to the grove of trees the trail made a bend. I rounded the bend and there in the trail was the pig's head grinning up at me with an evil look in his eyes. It was almost dark but I could still see him. For an instant I really thought I was a goner. The blood left my brain and I thought I was going to faint right on top of the pig. Then I started screaming and screaming. Sammy and Bailey were hiding nearby. They had really scared me. They laughed about this for a long time.

The New Well

We were all very healthy so it was a notable event when we all took sick at the same time. Dad being the biggest and strongest got the sickest.

It was determined the source of our illness was the water. The well was on the east side of the house. The corrals had good drainage. They were located to the west and south of the house. After a big rain they were washed clean and the water flooded across the flat below the house where the well was located.

The well was nine feet deep and on it was a windmill which pumped water into a large covered elevated tank which overflowed into a tall open tank on the ground. Nearby was a cement watering trough with a separate cement float box covered with heavy plank. There was another cement watering trough in the upper end of the horse corral. Half of the trough was in the adjoining cow pen with a covered float box in the middle under the corral fence.

The house water came from the elevated tank next to the windmill and was gravity fed which gave us modest pressure. Joe Yarborough lived at Fairbank across the highway from the headquarters. He was the Company windmill man and kept all the windmills on the Company in good working condition. So Joe was called to move the windmill and tank to the well location just south of the big cottonwood tree.

The septic tank was moved to the southwest corner outside of the yard fence. A fence was built around it so no one could drive over it.

This cured the problem.

Building a "Fire"

There were some things you did or didn't do around our house. Here are just a few of them. You got dressed in the morning when you got up and you didn't leave your room until the bed was made, your clothes put away and everything was in its place. Your hair was combed and you were washed up before coming out among the rest of the family and before coming to the table. This was to instill in us a sense of dignity and self respect.

There was no going around with your mouth hanging open and saying "Huh?" if you didn't hear or understand something. That's when you politely said, "Pardon me." No dragging your feet when you walked and no dawdling while you were doing your work. And you must have a reasonably good disposition. Above all, you never had to be reminded to do your chores. And of course, if you were told to do something, you did it immediately.

You knew the law. If you slipped up Dad never said a word to you. Suddenly you found yourself having a "fire" built under you. After a few "fires" your attitude and memory improved immensely. I can remember a few times when I had a "fire" built under me and it did me a world of good and taught me responsibility.

Dad treated his horses much like he did us kids. When we were riding and his horse didn't pay attention or got lazy, he got a "fire" built under him.

There is a lot to be said for this "fire" building. It contributed greatly to the peace and tranquillity around our house. There was never any of this "If I have to tell you one more time," or "I don't want to have to tell you again," or "How many times do I have to tell you?" or "I thought I told you to......."

Dad raised good kids and he had good horses.

Roughhousing on Horseback

When the Sammy and Bailey rode with Dad, they were working and their horses were saddled but there were the evenings when they rode for pleasure. The first thing the boys did was to break their horses to ride bareback. So if I wanted to go with them I rode bareback too. They didn't allow me to hold on to the horse's mane.

One day they put me on a little black horse called Chino and off we all went in a run. He had a kinky mane - what there was of it - and a kinky tail. I tried not to hold on but I didn't want to fall off either. So when the boys weren't looking I grabbed a handful of Chino's mane. It came out in my hand. There was something wrong with this horse. That's why the boys gave me Chino to ride. I had been set up and the boys had a good laugh when I pulled out Chino's mane. After that I didn't hold on.

Then there were times when we rode out of the horse pasture with our horses saddled. There was a lot of play in the boys. One would ride up to the other and say "Howdy do!" while taking off his hat and "accidentally" hitting the other boy's horse in the face. Sometimes this caused a wild ride. They didn't do this to me but there were other things they did.

If I was riding Stranger, the boys rode in the black brush hills where there were lots of gullies and bushes. Their horses jumped the gullies and dodged the bushes. Stranger jumped the gullies and the bushes. Every time he jumped he landed bucking. Sometimes I stayed on and sometimes I didn't.

When we got close to the river Sammy and Bailey would make

141

a run for it - crossing the river in a great splash of water. I tried to keep up but I was always a horse length behind and I would get hit with a wall of water.

One time I was riding a big lumpy horse named Tuffy and he tended to be on the lazy side. He stopped and wouldn't go so I kicked him - no luck. I pulled my piggin' string off my saddle and used it to give him a good whipping - no luck. Then I heard Sammy laughing. I looked back and there was Sammy with Tuffy's tail dallied around his saddle horn. No wonder Tuffy didn't move - he couldn't. Then I felt bad for whipping him.

Dad didn't tolerate much tom foolery so we had to be careful. Dad was in the lead and the boys and I were following behind him. Sammy grabbed a bunch of green mesquite beans and threw them to me and I threw them to Bailey. We did this for a while and then instead of Sammy throwing the mesquite beans to me, he threw them and hit my horse in the flank. I got bucked off and all of us were in trouble. I didn't care what the boys did to me. I just wanted to go with them. They weren't too rough on me and it was all in fun.

Sammy's Temper

All of us kids had tempers that we found hard to control. I think it had something to do with being a Foster. Mary and Sammy were slow to anger but when they lost their tempers they were a long time getting over it. Bailey and I , on the other hand, lost our tempers quickly and just as quickly we were over it.

It seems that one day Sammy and Bailey decided to make themselves a sling shot. They cut a couple of green forks out of a mesquite tree and used strips from an old inner tube and the tongues from an old pair of shoes to make two dandy sling shots.

They hung their new sling shots over their heads with the yoke resting on their chests. Bailey, in a playful mood and without a second thought, grabbed the bottom of Sammy's sling shot, pulled it down and released it. The fork caught Sammy under the chin and dropped him to the ground. That's when Sammy lost his temper. He came up off of the ground intending to do Bailey bodily harm but Bailey escaped. Then the hunt was on.

Sammy armed himself with a bow and arrow that had a horseshoe nail on the end for an arrowhead. Later the arrows would have an empty 30-30 casing with a nail driven through it. Nevertheless, the arrows with the horseshoe nails were pretty wicked for a ten year old.

Sammy's temper wouldn't cool down and the hunt went on for days. Only the four of us kids knew what was really going on. A truce was called at mealtime and at night since the boys shared a bed on the front porch. As soon as the coast was clear the hunt resumed. Above all, this had to be kept from Dad.

There was no reasoning with Sammy. Mary and I protected Bailey. He would slip into the house where Mary would feed him while I kept watch. Then he went back outside where he was on his own. There was lots of country out there.

Finally Sammy saw Bailey heading for the back door. Bailey hid behind the cooler but he forgot his legs weren't hidden. Sammy put an arrow in the bow and shot Bailey in the thigh. As soon as Sammy saw the terrible thing he had done to Bailey, his temper fit was over and in it's place was deep remorse. He pulled the arrow out of Bailey's leg, doctored him and took care of him the best he could.

Bailey forgave Sammy and they made a pact not to tell Dad.

Handwork

As young ladies, Mary and I were required to learn all our embroidery stitches and all the sewing stitches that were done by hand. This included darning socks and mending. We also learned to sew our clothes and household items on the treadle sewing machine. We had to either knit or crochet. Mary chose crocheting so I chose knitting. Mary was a whiz at crocheting as Mom helped her. No one helped me learn to knit. I was just given a book. I did learn to knit but my heart really wasn't in it.

Mom was an expert at all types of handwork. She made lots of dollies, lace edgings for handkerchiefs out of sewing thread and she also tatted. It seemed there was nothing she couldn't do. She even knit her own socks. That was something that did spark my interest but Mom said it was too difficult for me but she did teach Mary to knit socks in secret. I didn't know this until I was grown and old. It was then that a nice neighbor helped me learn to knit socks. Learning is a lot easier when you're young.

It was considered unseemly for a young girl to sleep on a plain pillow case so I embroidered my pillow case and Mary graciously crocheted an edging for me which I then sewed on. I had met my pillow case requirement.

Mary had a large and beautiful hope chest when she got married. I didn't even start one. I said I would never marry. I wanted to get an education and be a school teacher - hopefully in a country school.

Laundry

We washed the laundry in the kitchen in front of the sink, winter and summer alike. We brought in a wooden bench to set the wash tubs on. One for washing and one for rinsing. The wood stove had a water jacket in the fire box. Water circulated by convection through this into a galvanized hot water tank so when there was a fire in the stove we had hot running water in the sink and bathroom. We used a bucket to fill the tubs with water.

Wash day came once a week. All the clothes, bedding and towels were washed on the rub board. Mary washed and wrung the clothes from the wash tub into the rinse tub and I rinsed and wrung them as dry as I could. We both hung them on the clothesline on the east side of the house. We cooked starch on the stove and poured it into a bucket. Everything that would be ironed was run through the starch bucket after being rinsed.

I washed my own clothes. I also washed all the socks and handkerchiefs. Dad felt since I was young and my hands were small I wouldn't rub the skin off my knuckles while washing the small items. Not true.

As soon as the laundry was dry we brought it in the house, made the beds, folded what needed to be folded and sprinkled the ironing. The ironing was done the next day. We used a set of three sad irons heated on the wood stove. Mary and I each ironed our own clothes and divided up the household ironing and Dad's and the boys' clothes. After everything was ironed, we mended. There were always socks to darn.

As I sat there darning socks I made myself a promise. I would never wear socks when I was grown.

Flour Sacks and Salt Sacks

Our flour came in twenty five pound sacks and we used a lot of flour. Dad wanted hot bread with every meal so that meant lots of pancakes, biscuits and cornbread. He would eat yeast bread but only when it was hot and fresh from the oven. But being a cowboy, biscuits and cornbread were close to his heart.

The flour sacks were sewn with a chain stitch. When a sack was emptied we took it outside, turned it wrong side out and pulled the string holding it together. Then after a good shake it went into the wash. The printing on the flour sacks was easily washed out. These sacks were soft and closely woven and made excellent dish towels and aprons.

Mary and Mom crocheted our "dish clothes" from string or crochet thread called bedspread cotton. We could no longer refer to them as "dish rags" as they weren't rags but works of art.

The Company put out a coarse mineralized pink salt in heavy plank troughs for the cattle. This salt was made by Morton. We could wash out the blue print but the word Morton was red and hard to wash out. While Mary was at home she knew how to get all the lettering out. I guess I must have been riding with Dad and the boys when Mary did the salt sacks. She didn't keep me home to help so I didn't learn how. After Mary left home, I washed and bleached the salt sacks but the word Morton was still visible.

There were a lot of sacks all washed and neatly folded so Dad loaded them in the car and took them to Tombstone to Mrs. Elliott's house. She was an older woman and said she could get the sacks white and she did. She quilted a lot so Dad gave her half of the salt sacks for her labor.

Salt for the cattle came in one hundred pound sacks. The sacks were coarsely woven and very strong and durable. We used every sack we had. We sewed them together on the treadle sewing machine with double seams so they wouldn't ravel. All of our bed linens and curtains were made out of these sacks. We used Ritz dye and dyed the curtains but the sheets and pillow cases were left white. It took quite a few sacks to make a sheet and it had lots of seams in it. We didn't mind the seams. At least we had sheets on our beds. Mom and Dad had real store bought sheets. I guess, Mom being a Yankee and from the East she wanted something a little smoother. We saved and used everything we could. This made our lives better and more comfortable.

Chores

In the beginning Sammy and Bailey were supposed to trade chores every week as chopping wood was harder and took longer than the corral chores. But before long Sammy did the corral chores and Bailey chopped wood and this was agreeable to them both. Of course, the corral chores were more fun but they had to be done on time twice a day. Chopping wood could be done anytime as long as the wood box was heaped full at night. This suited Bailey and he quite often had a pile of wood chopped ahead of time ready to be brought to the house at night.

Mary took care of the house and the cooking. It was my job to set the table and do anything Mary told me to do. Sometimes this was making the biscuits, cutting the meat or peeling potatoes. We both did the dishes and we took turns washing and drying. The kitchen was cleaned after every meal and the house was always neat. If you used something you put it back when you were finished.

We were all responsible for keeping our rooms clean and our beds made. Mary and I shared a room and slept together. The boys slept together on the front porch. Their bed was like a bedroll with a heavy canvas tarp that ran under the mattress and back over the top of the bed. This protected the boys and the bed from the weather. We all had to have our rooms clean and our beds made before we came out in the morning.

It was my job to take care of the chickens and feed the pig. I kept the kerosene jug full and brought in a bucket of chips every

151

night to start the fires with. And taking out the ashes and trash
every day was also part of my chores.

The Milk Cow

Each camp had two milk cows so one would always be fresh. They were dairy stock, although for a little while we had a Hereford cow named Molly that gave a fair amount of milk. Milking was always done at five o'clock in the morning and five o'clock in the evening. The cow was fed a gallon of cottonseed cake pellets while she was being milked. During the day she was turned out into the horse pasture and at night she was left in the cow pen and given alfalfa hay. The milk pen calf was turned out into the horse trap between milkings and was also given hay. The horse trap was a small pasture attached to the barn and corrals.

We got a gallon of milk twice a day. This was about half of what the cow gave. The calf got the rest. Our sugar came in cloth sacks and these were used to strain the milk. The milk was then put in the gunny sack cooler and after setting overnight we took a ladle and dipped the cream into a large crock. When the crock was full, it was churned into butter. Then the butter was washed and salted and the buttermilk put in the cooler and used to drink or make biscuits. Some of the skimmed milk was allowed to sour (clabber) and this was made into cottage cheese. It was poured into a large pan and warmed on the back of the wood stove. When the curds separated from the whey and were barely firm it was poured into a sugar sack, washed and hung on the clothesline to dry. Cream was added and it was ready for the table.

The cow was a very important part of our food supply. She provided us with milk, butter, buttermilk, cream, whipping cream and cottage cheese. The surplus milk was fed to the pig. The cow even contributed to mice control as the barn cats were given a sardine can full of milk at each milking before it was brought to the house. This was the only food we gave the cats. The rest of their diet they had to catch. The milk pen calf was butchered for meat. The cow manure was used in the vegetable garden.

We were very careful with the milk containers. Everything was washed in hot soapy water, rinsed and hung outside on the "milk tree" so the sun could sanitize them. This included a seamless aluminum milk bucket. There was even a wire line for the straining cloth. The "milk tree" was a well-branched mesquite tree with the bark removed and the branches cut to make pegs. This was planted in the yard between the house and the gate.

The cow was pretty good about coming home at night to be milked. If she wasn't there she came when called. Every time she was called, she answered. If she didn't answer, she wasn't going to come home and you had to go get her either on horseback or on foot. If she did this too many times we put a bell on her so she would be easy to find. Most cows and milk cows in particular can be contrary from time to time when they have a mind to.

Tadpoles

There were lots of frogs in the river and all summer the river was full of tadpoles. I had two frog farms - one in each of the watering troughs. Then as they matured into young frogs I returned them to the river. I loved frogs. There were lots of toads too and they showed up at the water's edged on the river during the rainy season. But I didn't bring these home.

Mom was very particular about the quantity of milk that was brought to the house. It should be a gallon at each milking. This was easy to do as we only milked the right side and the calf got the left side. When we got all the milk we could, the calf was turned in and with one hand on his nose he was guided to suck just a little from each teat. This made the cow "give down" the rest of the milk. This was where most of the cream was.

Sometimes the boys mixed work with play and they let the calf have too much and there wasn't enough milk. So they dipped the milk bucket into the watering trough and brought the level up where it should be. No one would have known about this if one night some of my tadpoles hadn't found their way into the milk bucket. When Mary strained the milk, she found the tadpoles.

Dad laid down the law - no more watering the milk.

Chickens

I loved chickens and taking care of them was my job. These were no ordinary chickens. They were game chickens. They had never been caged. They roamed free and nested wherever they chose. An exact count was never made but Dad could look over the flock at feeding time and know if one of the hens was missing. I would guess there were at least twenty hens. There was one rooster and lots of chicks from just hatched to fryer size. We ate the young roosters and the pullets went back into the flock. Mom ate the old hens. She loved boiled chicken.

I fed the chickens milo maize at chore time in the evening. When they were called, they came from everywhere - some even flying over the corral fence. These chickens were next to wild with good survivor skills. A mother hen with chicks could be formidable. No dog or cat dared venture too close - people either for that matter.

Once we saw a hen with small chicks fly into the air to do battle with a chicken hawk. Another time a hen with baby chicks was out in the sacaton flat when the ramuda of horses went through. She put up a fight and the horses went around her and the chicks. The hens were terrific mothers and hid their nests well.

When a lone hen came into the corral about mid-morning looking for something to eat and clucking, you knew she was setting. I would feed her and then hide so she couldn't see me. When she finished eating she went back to her nest which could be some distance from the corral. If she saw me or thought she was being followed she would go everywhere except to her nest. Sometimes it would take several tries before I found the nest. Then all the eggs were marked and the hatch time was marked on the calendar. A hen was always set on an uneven number of eggs, nine or eleven. Periodically the nest was checked to see if another hen was laying in the same nest. These new eggs would be unmarked and went to the house. Setting hens were mean and fiercely protected their nests.

Game chickens were almost varmint-proof. It was survival of the fittest. They roosted high in the mesquite trees. Dad put a couple of nest boxes in the trees close to the corral to encourage some of the hens to lay there so we would have eggs for the house. There was always a surplus of chickens but never a surplus of eggs.

There were always two adult roosters. One ran free with the hens and the other was in jail. Dad built a cage about four feet by four feet by four feet and suspended it on the inside of the hay barn. This cage had wooden bars and looked like a jail. Every day Dad took this rooster out and exercised him on a couple of hay bales. With just the touch of Dad's fingertips the rooster ran sideways, forwards, backwards and did somersaults in the air. It was amazing to watch.

Dad used to fight roosters and always kept his roosters in top condition. When a young rooster reached adulthood, his comb and wattles were trimmed so another rooster would have nothing to peck and hold onto. This made the rooster look like a warrior.

Mom was very particular with her sewing scissors but she did allow Dad to use them for trimming the rooster's combs. I held the rooster while Dad did the cutting. The rooster didn't flinch. He just blinked his eyes and occasionally shook his head, splattering blood all over Dad and me. Next came the spurs.

These were sawed off close to the leg with a special saw. This was so he couldn't hurt another rooster in a fight and also he would be ready to wear the gaffs in a real fight.

Dad had a small green metal box in which he kept his cock fighting equipment. There were gaffs shaped like long curved knives and some like long needles. There were small buckskin pouches filled with cotton to be worn over the gaffs to protect the handler until fight time. This is where he kept the spur saw and the toe punch to mark baby chicks. There were also colored leg bands to mark adult birds. I never saw a real cock fight. I think Dad gave this up after Bailey and I were born. He paid Sammy's doctor and hospital bill when he was born with his winnings from a cock fight.

Of course, there was a surplus of good roosters which were put out on a "walk" with some of Dad's friends who also kept game chickens. From time to time these roosters were rotated. All of Dad's roosters were named Caesar but the hens were unnamed.

One of the most important things I did was take the hen off the nest as soon as the last chick hatched and bring them all to the horse trough where each chick was given their first drink. A shallow pan of water was kept full by the trough for the baby chicks so they wouldn't drown trying to get a drink out of the trough. As soon as they started to feather-out they could swim and could get out of the water by themselves if they fell in. After their first drink, the hen took care of them without further help until they were fully feathered and could take care of themselves.

We had a long wire hook we used to catch chickens with and we tried to catch chickens when the rooster wasn't there. He protected the flock and would fight anything or anyone bothering one of the chickens, especially one of the hens. Dad or the boys killed the fryers by chopping off their heads with an axe. As soon as they quit flopping, Mary and I picked and cleaned them. Then it was into the frying pan. This was our company dinner along with mashed potatoes and gravy.

All of us loved fried chicken but none of us quite as much as Bailey. To Bailey each piece of chicken was as good as the next. The neck was just as good as the wishbone.

The chickens added a lot to our lives and I felt privileged to be entrusted with their care.

Buena School

When we moved back to the Wolf Place we went to school at Buena. At that time there were enough children to have two teachers - four grades in each room. One bus - an older pickup with a homemade camper was driven by one of the school board members, Mike Richards. He picked up the kids on the Huachuca Strip and also the kids in Fry. Sometimes his wife drove the bus. The other bus was a dark blue two-seated car with a School Bus sign on the back. This bus was driven by Mrs. Schrader.. She was also the post mistress at the Fry post office. She picked up us four Fosters at the Wolf Place, two girls at Louis Springs and three Castros at Charleston. I don't know how we all fit in but we did.

The Backrichs drove themselves to school. The older ones dropped off the younger ones, Gwen and George, on their way to high school in Tombstone. If for some reason George didn't have a way to school he rode their old horse to school and put him in a small fenced-in triangle where the roads came together. George was the first one to get to school and the last one to leave.

We had running water at the school, two bathrooms and two drinking fountains. The water came from a well and windmill in front of the school. We were allowed to climb up the windmill tower and slide down the pipe.

While sliding down the pipe one day I tried to avoid landing on the honey bees getting a drink on a steel plate attached to the pipe about a foot off the ground. I thought I could push myself clear of the steel plate and land on the ground. I miscalculated and took a fair amount of hide and meat off my shin. It was no big deal. My sister took care of me. The teacher didn't worry about anything on the playground. The older kids looked after the younger ones just like they did at home.

The school was heated with butane. Each classroom had a heater. There was an extra room with a rough floor called the shop with a hammer, nails, saw, pliers and probably a few other tools. The older boys took care of any repairs.

There was a nest of honey bees in the attic and once a year Mrs. Bledsoe declared a holiday. The older boys robbed the bees and the girls put the honey comb into a large pot and heated it on a gas hot plate in the office used by the teachers to heat their soup on. As the honey melted all the wax, bee bread, bee larva and dead bees floated to the top and were skimmed off leaving nothing but clean honey. I don't remember anyone ever getting stung by a bee. While all this was going on Mrs. Bledsoe drove two miles into Fry and bought bread and butter. Then the entire school sat under the ramada and ate bread, butter and honey for the rest of the day.

We all brought our lunch to school and most of us ate under the ramada at the picnic table. Jimmy Diak ate alone preferring his own company to that of the other kids. His lunch was always the same - thick bolonga on fresh soft white store bought bread. This was the best sandwich any of us had ever seen. The Mexican girls from Louis Springs always brought tortillas and beans. We Fosters always brought two biscuits with cherry preserves. Jimmy would much rather have the tortillas and beans so he asked Bailey if he could arrange a trade. Well, the little Mexican girls didn't think too much of bolonga but they did like biscuits. So a three-way trade was made. Everyday at noon Bailey traded his two biscuits for two tortillas and beans. Next he traded the tortillas and beans for the bolonga sandwich. When this was done Bailey brought me the bolonga sandwich and he ate my biscuits. I knew how much Bailey would have liked to have eaten that sandwich but he insisted I eat it. This was something only a twin would do.

In the fall Mrs. Bledsoe drove down to the Wolf Place to see Dad. She told him to keep Sammy and Bailey home from school while the roundup was camped at the house. They would learn a lot more from the roundup than they would at school. She said they just sat in school looking out the window wishing they were helping with the roundup. They were given extra work and excused from school as long as the fall roundup was at the Wolf Place.

Every spring both boys were given extra work and finished up the school year early so they could go with the spring roundup.

Sammy and Bailey were both in the eighth grade and Sammy had been hired as the Company horse wrangler for the spring works. The wagon was camped at the Horse Camp in the Dragoon Mountains when school let out for the summer. Sammy and Bailey were driven home to attend their eighth grade graduation.

The playground equipment at Buena School consisted of a set of teeter-totters and a swing set. The Buena School Board bought a merry-go-round and had it installed. All of the kids were happy with the new merry-go-round but when we played on it, it fell over. Mrs. Bledsoe reported this to the School Board. She told them she had some little boys that could install the merry-go-round properly.

So Sammy, Bailey and George Bakarich were called upon to do the job. They had dug lots of post holes so they dug a deep hole, mixed cement and set the support post. The merry-go-round had to be disassembled for this. After allowing enough time for the cement to set the merry-go-round was reassembled and ready to use.

The three boys were excused from school to work on the merry-go-round but when recess time came they were to play with the other kids. When the bell rang they went back to work.

They did a great job and the merry-go-round held up to all the use we could give it. When school let out for the summer the boys disassembled it and reassembled it in the fall. We all loved the merry-go-round and took good care of it.

Mrs. Bledsoe spent a lot of time with the eighth graders. They were taught state and federal government and given sample ballets to vote in the primary and general elections. They were taught how to write checks and balance a check book. In those days not all the kids would go on to high school so they were taught as much as possible how to function in the world.

Mrs. Bledsoe not only taught us our school lessons she taught us a few lessons about life. She told us we were getting two new students. They were Jewish children, a brother and a sister. We were to be nice to them and make them welcome. She warned us that they would be eating food that was strange to us - different from what the rest of us ate. Above all, we were not to discriminate against them.

Sure enough here came a boy and girl just older than myself. They were so different from us country kids. They were soft, white and pudgy. The girl wore long white stockings and a white blouse with a black velvet skirt and jacket. The boy dressed in black velvet knee pants and jacket with a white shirt and white stockings. They dressed like this every day. They stayed to themselves and never went outside. They didn't eat with the rest of us and they ate food unfamiliar to us. They were pampered children. We treated them politely but they weren't friendly. It would be years before I realized it was they that discriminated against the rest of us.

164

Our numbers dwindled and all eight grades were in one room. Mrs. Bledsoe didn't like history or geography so she just skipped them. Then toward the end of the school year all eight grades had two days of nothing but history and two days of nothing but geography. When we got into high school we were no better and no worse than our town counterparts in history and geography. Mrs. Bledsoe may not have cared much for history or geography but she loved English. We all knew our parts of speech and how to diagram a sentence. Then there was literature. We read all the classics and memorized Longfellow, Whittier and other great poets. I still have the English Handbook she gave me when I graduated from the eighth grade.

Life Magazine, Saturday Evening Post and National Geographic were kept on the table in the back of the room along with a good assortment of comic books. When we finished our work we could go to this table and read anything we chose. Our teacher said she didn't care what we read for pleasure as long as we read. She was confident that as our reading skill improved so would our taste in reading. And she was right.

When the older students finished their work they could listen to the younger children read. This was a privilege. If anyone had trouble in math they were sent into an empty classroom with me until they mastered fractions, decimals or whatever. I was a whiz at math. No student failed any subject. If they had trouble they were given extra help until they learned.

One year the Buena School District hired Bailey to water the iris and poppies in front of the school twice a week for the summer. To do this Bailey rode horseback the eight miles to the school. I felt so bad for Bailey to be alone so I went with him. We were used to riding but not like this. It's one thing to ride across country and quite another to ride on a road. It was monotonous. Even the horses felt it.

We started out early in the morning and when we got to
the school we got a drink of water and Bailey watered all the
flowers which took a lot of time with one hose and not too much
water pressure. When this was done we rode on into Fry which
was another two miles. We got the mail and Bailey put it in a
gunnysack and tied it to the horn of his saddle. Mom subscribed
to the Phoenix Republic newspaper so there was quite a lot of
mail. Then we rode home. This made a twenty mile ride. We
didn't take anything to eat or drink so we were hungry when we
pulled the saddles off our horses and went to the house.

There is a strange thing that happens when you spend a long
time in the saddle. When you get off your horse you feel like you
are only two feet tall - sort of like Alice in Wonderland. By the
time you unsaddle your horse and walk to the house you have
regained your normal height. This never failed to amaze me.

Mrs. Bledsoe was a wonderful teacher and took a personal
interest in each of her students. She worked with Mary and got
her to the grade level she should be and she advanced Bailey
and Sammy one year ahead. All the moving around earlier had
caused all of us except me to lose one or more grades. She was
my model for a teacher.

In 1952, a year after I graduated there was an increase in the
population of Fry. Another teacher was hired to teach the first
four grades. She was Mrs. Johnson and had taught when we first
went to Buena. Mrs. Bledsoe taught the fifth through the eighth.
Even a custodian was hired. The truck with the homemade
camper that served as a bus was replaced with a modern van - still
driven by Mike Richards. The River Bus stayed the same - a car
driven by Mrs. Shader. There were fewer children from the river.
It was in 1952, that Buena School published it's first annual. That
was the year Sammy and Bailey graduated from the eighth grade.

One of the neat things about going to a one room school is

that the younger kids listened in on the lessons being taught to the older kids and learned a lot by accident.

Cornbread

When I was eight years old, Dad sent me into the kitchen to make pancakes for breakfast. He said Mary was tired and so was he. It was about time I learned to cook. I had seen pancakes made many times so with a few instructions I had no trouble getting breakfast. After that I could cook breakfast whenever I had to.

Next came biscuits. This was more difficult but with time and practice I mastered the art of biscuit making. I have to say we all made outstanding biscuits - real cowboy biscuits.

When Dad made biscuits, he made them Texas style. The end result was the same but the technique was different. Whereas, we made the dough in a bowl, he made the dough in the sack of flour. At that time flour came in a twenty five pound cloth sack. He rolled down the cloth flour sack and made a well in the flour. Next he put everything in the well and carefully stirred it up. Everything that stuck together was biscuit dough. Then he rolled out the dough and cut out the biscuits with a drinking glass or just pinched off a piece of dough, rolled it into a ball, flattened it and turned it over in a greased pan. For a rolling pin Dad used a round whiskey bottle. Later we did have a wooden rolling pin but he broke off one handle so it would still have the same feel as the whiskey bottle.

Dad never did allow us to make biscuits Texas style as he figured we would probably ruin the whole sack of flour.

Then the day came when I was nine years old and Dad sent me into the kitchen to make cornbread. I asked for a recipe but he said, "No." He didn't believe in recipes. You just went into the kitchen and cooked. He said just start out like you are going to make biscuits only leave out half of the flour and put in cornmeal instead. And I did exactly that.

So far there was nothing Mary and I cooked that Sammy and Bailey wouldn't eat even if it was burned. Well, when my cornbread came out of the oven the boys refused to eat it. They gave it to Shep, but not even the dog would eat it. Finally, it was given to the pig and he ate it.

After that Dad did allow me to use a recipe for cornbread.

Jimmy's Biscuits

Mom's younger sister, Ruth Diak, found herself out of work and needed a place to stay until she got another job. So she and her ten year old son moved in with us.

Jimmy was an only child and used to being the center of attention and having his own way and not sharing. Even at that things weren't too bad except for a couple of incidents.

Jimmy didn't work or do chores like the rest of us. He had a red wagon and it would have been very helpful if it could be used to bring wood to the house. But as he pointed out it was his and it wasn't going to be used to haul wood. This really upset Dad but he kept his temper.

And of course, there was the thing about chicken. Eating chicken was a treat for us usually reserved for when we had company. But Dad allowed us to have chicken fairly often while Ruth and Jimmy were guests in our house. Like most kids we liked to get the wishbone and took turns having it. It seems Jimmy would eat only white meat and especially liked the wishbone. This didn't set too well with us kids but chicken was a special treat and we enjoyed whichever piece we got. All of us that is except Bailey. He enjoyed every single piece of the chicken even the neck and ate it with gusto.

Jimmy having to have the wishbone all the time really got to Dad. After all these were his game chickens we were eating. But still Dad kept his temper. I don't think us kids had ever seen Dad so good at keeping his temper.

One evening we were all sitting on the back porch talking when the subject of sourdough came up. Mary and I had been making sourdough biscuits and pancakes. Jimmy announced there was nothing hard about making sourdough biscuits so Dad invited him to make some for supper and he told Mary and I to stay out of the kitchen. We all knew Jimmy couldn't cook and we waited to see just how bad these biscuits were going to be. I think we had all had about enough of Jimmy.

Well, Jimmy went into the kitchen with an air of confidence. There was a lot of noise coming from the kitchen and a lot of time went by. Finally we heard him whacking and pounding the dough with the rolling pin. He was unknowingly providing us with a great deal of entertainment. At last he came out to tell us the biscuits were out of the oven. We absolutely could not believe these biscuits. They were the best. I think he even outdid Dad's biscuits. Certainly there was no justice that day.

Ruth got a job at Nick's Place and she and Jimmy left and our lives returned to normal.

Invincible

One morning I woke up feeling really, really good. Never before had I felt this good. I was invincible. Today was the day to settle the score with Mary for all past grievances. But Mary had other ideas. She too woke up feeling really good, only she was in a good mood and wanted no part of putting me in my place. But I was persistent. Finally Mary gave in and was giving me a good boxing. All my invincibility was gone and I was getting the worst of it. The only thing left to do was run.

I was a fast runner but Mary was faster. I had a plan. Out across the sacaton flat I ran. I figured I was smaller and more nimble and I could manage the sacaton clumps better than Mary. My plan was flawed. Mary could still run faster than me even in the sacaton clumps. When I knew I was going to be caught, I threw myself down onto my back in a clearing in the sacaton and began kicking so Mary couldn't get close to me. My reasoning was flawed too. Mary just waited until I was too tired to put up a struggle. Then she move in and showed me no mercy.

Whenever Mary did something, she was thorough. That was the last time Mary and I quarreled or came to blows.

Giggles

One night at the supper table one of us kids got the giggles and before long we all had them. This was the first and the last time we had the giggles around Dad. He had absolutely no patience with silliness.

Suddenly everything was funny, even Dad scolding us and our fear of him. We laughed and laughed. Every time we tried to sober up it just made matters worse. Even when Dad slammed his fist down on the table and we just about jumped out of our hides, we just laughed that much harder. Clearly the situation was out of control.

Finally in desperation Dad took us outside. We were all sure we were going to get the spanking of our lives and still we laughed. We were relieved when all he did was put each of us in a corner of the yard until we could sober up. It took awhile. I'm not sure we got supper that night.

The Game of Murder

I t was always fun when the Hunts came over. When other people came to visit we played hide and go seek when it got dark. But when the Hunts came over we played Murder. This was a game Donnie taught us. She probably brought it with her from the East. We never played Murder with anyone else. It was reserved exclusively for the Hunts.

Many young wealthy girls came out West and married cowboys. Donnie fell into this category. She was small, freckled faced with red hair and the kindest most bubbly personality. Everyone loved Donnie. Lonnie was Dad's best friend. He was nice looking, short and had very dark eyes that always twinkled. He and Donnie were a matched pair. They had two children. Nancy looked like her father and she was Mary's age. Happy was just like his name implied. He looked like Donnie and he was Sammy's age. They called their parents by their given names.

We loved the game of Murder and it went something like this. A small piece of paper for each player was folded and put into a hat. All the papers were blank except two. One was marked M for Murder and the other was marked D. A. for District Attorney. We all drew a piece of paper out of the hat and carefully looked at it so no one could see. Only the D. A. declared himself and he stayed in the house with the adults.

The rest of us went outside in the dark. There we walked around by ourselves - no pairing up. We had to give the Murderer a chance to strike without a witness. We became afraid of everyone because we knew a murderer walked among us. When

175

we met and passed someone we were surprised and relieved when we didn't become a victim. When the Murderer picked a victim and the opportunity was right he quietly whispered "You're dead." Then you laid down on the ground and waited to be found. The person finding you cried, "Murder!" and we all went into the house.

Only the victim knew who killed him and of course, they could say nothing. The D. A. began questioning everyone as to their whereabouts and so forth. Everyone had to tell the truth except the Murderer. He could lie. The adults were the audience. I think they enjoyed the game as much as the kids. Finally when the D. A. thought he had solved the case he accused the person of murder. At this point the Murderer had to confess. Usually the D. A. was right but not always. This ended the game and it was time to play another.

Charlie and I

I was very shy and hid when company came especially if there were any boys. They liked to tease me and pull my pigtails. I was small and skinny and I could fold myself up and hide almost anywhere - under the bed, on the closet shelf, behind the dresser, in a dresser drawer. I was good at hiding.

One day Donnie Hunt came by in the jeep. She had her daughter, Nancy, and Nancy's friend, Emma Mae, with her. They were going to the Escapules for a picnic and they had come by to pick up Mary. It seems the purpose of the picnic was for the girls to see Charlie. It was decided I could go too.

I was eleven years old and I didn't go anywhere I didn't have to unless I had Mary with me. Then I stayed close to her never letting her get more than a foot away from me.

Charlie was eighteen and very nice looking. He was German and French on his father's side and English and Irish on his mother's. Charlie was farming and had the river dammed up for irrigation. That made this part of the river a nice place for a picnic and a good place for everyone to swim.

When it came time to eat, Mary fixed herself and me a plate and we sat down on a pair of chaps to have our lunch. I was a slow eater and before I knew it Mary had cleaned her plate and had gone back for seconds leaving me alone. I was upset with Mary for leaving me but there wasn't anything I could do but sit still and wait for her to return and hope nobody noticed me. About this time, here came Charlie and asked if he could eat lunch with me. I really wished he wouldn't but there was nothing

I could do but politely accept. I sat very still but Charlie didn't tease me. He was quiet and kind and before long I relaxed. We talked and ate our lunch.

Soon the picnic was over and we were on our way home. I didn't think about Charlie again until he came to see my sister when she was sixteen.

There was a full moon and Charlie brought over a telescope. He and Mary sat in the wagon under the big cottonwood tree and looked at the moon. Charlie even let me look too, then Mary sent me and Shep to the house. Neither of us wanted to go but Mary insisted.

Charlie joined the Navy and Mary got married to one of the Boquillas cowboys.

When Charlie came home on leave he always came by the house for a visit. I was still shy and avoided company whenever possible but for some reason I made an exception where Charlie was concerned. I really thought he came by to see the folks and I'm sure he did. I didn't realize it but Charlie had begun to watch over me.

Charlie in the Navy.

Mary at the Wolf Place.
Chicken house and out house are in the background.

Wolf Place. Gunny sack cooler on back porch.

Evenings

In the evenings after supper we hung a lantern on the yard gate post. This was home base - we were going to play hide and go seek. We never tired of this and it was even more fun if the Bakarichs came over. It was easy to hide in the dark and we usually went some distance from home base. Amazingly none of us got on a rattlesnake and there were plenty of them around.

When it was cold we stayed inside after dark. We had the living room to ourselves and shut the kitchen door so we didn't disturb Dad and Mom. The boys braided rawhide or mended a bridle while Mary read to us. I don't remember what I did except be wherever the other kids were. I always cried when Mary read "The Littlest Rebel" or "The Littlest Angel". These were good times spent around the table at night with just the four of us.

Dad loved his True Detective magazines. Mom read to him in their bedroom every night. She had the most wonderful voice and reading style. Sometimes she read late into the night. After Mary and I had gone to bed we would listen to these stories too since we had adjoining bedrooms.

These stories were morbid and gruesome. This is what we heard as we drifted off to sleep. I think Mary was unaffected by them - but not me. Lying there in the dark listening to these stories made the hair stand up on the back of my neck. No wonder I was afraid of the dark.

Once we had corn on the cob and the boys saved a couple of the cobs from the pig. They made corn cob pipes and even made

one for me. Someone had told them about smoking coffee.
So one evening Mary let the boys have some coffee for the corn
cob pipes. It stunk so bad - like burnt coffee and it smelled
up the whole house. We thought we were hiding it from Dad
because the door was closed. The boys smoked their pipes with
determination in spite of getting burned. The first time I sucked a
hot coal of coffee down my throat and got burned I was through
smoking.

Some evenings when Mom and Dad sat on the front steps
and we were all gathered around like a family, Mom sang. I don't
think she was singing to us so much as she was singing to Dad.
They were her songs from New England. She had a low soft voice
and she could really sing. She whistled too. This was a great way
to spend the evening. It made the world feel good.

But the best evenings of all were when Dad sat at the corner
of a small table in the kitchen with his legs crossed. Us kids sat
on the floor around him and he sang to us. He had a strong, deep,
wonderful voice. He sang the old ballads and some cowboy songs
too - some funny and some sad. Most of these songs are lost
now. He recited "The Shooting of Dan McGrew" and I don't think
anyone ever did it better. He could make us laugh or cry with his
songs. But when Sammy left home and Bailey right behind him
the singing stopped.

When the Others Left Home

Sammy turned thirteen in January and the following April the Company hired him as horse wrangler for the spring roundup. He would do a man's work and receive a man's pay. I was so proud of Sammy. It never occurred to me that he was leaving home. I thought he would just work through the roundup and come home when Dad did.

When the roundup was over, Sammy went to work for the Company as an extra man at another camp. I missed Sammy and I'm sure Bailey did too.

At home Bailey took over Sammy's chores and continued riding with Dad and helping him. There was always a horse for me and I rode too when Mary didn't need me.

The next year Mary got married and I did her work but I didn't stay in the house any longer than I had to. I wanted to spend all the time I could outside and horseback.

I was happy for Mary but I missed her a lot more than I thought I would. This was the first time I had ever slept alone and it was lonely at night without Mary. She had taken care of me most of my life. She was the one I turned to if I was troubled or wanted to know something or needed advice. Mary was a much bigger part of my life than I realized. At least I still had Bailey - but not for long. We didn't talk about it but I suppose Bailey went through a similar period of adjustment when Sammy left home.

Then when we turned fourteen in February, Bailey left home. He went to work on the spring roundup as a cowboy.

They already had a horse wrangler. This time I knew when the roundup was over Bailey wouldn't be coming home. And he didn't.

I took over Bailey's chores and rode with Dad everyday and wrestled calves. There were still screw worms so life was busy and there was lots of work. I didn't have much time to think about being lonely but I was.

I still saw the boys during the spring and fall roundup when the chuck wagon was camped at the house. But it was during the summer when Dad went on vacation that the boys came home.

The first year the Company sent Sammy to the Wolf Place to relieve Dad. Then the next year Sammy got his vacation and came home and Bailey relieved Dad. Dad always stayed home so we had the family together for two weeks. That is except for Mary. She and her husband were in New Mexico on the Victorio Cattle Company which was part of Boquillas.

Going Down the Rope

It was fall roundup and Bailey and I were home. A horse had been left in the horse pasture for transportation since neither of us could drive - we were only thirteen. There was always the possibility that Mom might need a doctor.

It was Sunday and no school so Bailey had gone riding. He came across an unbranded heifer. She had been missed in the spring and again in the fall. She was truly a maverick. That is she was unbranded and old enough that she was no longer following her mother.

Bailey drove her home and put her in the corral. He was going to brand her. Everything would have gone without a hitch if I hadn't decided to help. This animal was too big to flank so that meant going down the rope.

When it's done right there's nothing to it. The animal is roped by the head and then you run down the rope holding onto it with your right hand. As soon as you reach the animal you grab the right front leg with your left hand and lift up. When the calf sees you running toward him, he pulls back hard on the rope trying to get loose. As soon as you reach him you grab the right leg with your left hand and pull up hard. As soon as the calf feels you grab his leg he jumps and with this momentum he is easily thrown. Then with one knee on his neck and the other knee on his side you double the front leg back and with your other hand you grab as deep as you can in his flank. This keeps him from kicking. Now he is immobile and ready to be hog tied. Needless to say timing is everything. Never is it more true that he who hesitates is lost or in this case kicked and trampled or both.

Bailey roped the heifer by the head and I went down the rope. When I was head to head with her I couldn't believe how big she was. I hesitated. In that moment I lost the advantage - the element of surprise. When I grabbed her front leg she was no longer pulling back on the rope. She jumped and kicked me completely across the corral. Her foot caught me on the eye socket on the side of my face cutting it open. So Bailey jumped off his horse, ran down the rope and did it right.

The next morning one of my eyes was swelled shut and looked like a plum and the other one wasn't much better but I could see out of it a little bit. I really, really wanted to stay home from school for a day or two. But Mom said, "No". I wished I had a pair of sunglasses but I didn't.

Bailey was in the eighth grade at Buena and I was in my first year of high school in Tombstone. I knew that this day I would face the world alone. So with all the courage and dignity I could muster I boarded the bus for the long ride to Tombstone.

Old Good Eye

The first time I saw Old Good Eye, a cowboy had dropped him off at the house while he went on the fall roundup. Old Good Eye was a Dalmatian dog with one white eye and one brown eye. He was blind in the white eye and so the name of Old Good Eye. He was a big friendly dog but he was a glutton and would eat just about anything.

The linoleum had been replaced on the kitchen floor and the old linoleum was outside the yard fence by the trash barrels. And sure enough, there was Old Good Eye tearing off pieces of the linoleum and gulping it down.

After breakfast the leftover pancake batter was cooked and fed to the dogs. One cold frosty morning, Mary cooked the leftover batter and sent Bailey out the door with the hot pancakes for the dogs. He tossed the first one to Shep who caught it and gently laid it down in front of his feet to cool. The next pancake went to Old Good Eye. He caught it and swallowed it without hesitation. This went on until all the pancakes were gone.

Suddenly Old Good Eye sat down and began to howl. Then yelping and howling he took off across the sacaton flat like he was on fire. He ran in bigger and bigger circles. Then he stopped, put his head down and then trotted back to the house to see if there was something else to eat. Out in the sacaton flat, the steam was rising where Old Good Eye had left his pancakes.

The fall roundup ended and the cowboy returned and picked up his dog. He went to work for the Lucky Hills Ranch just outside of Tombstone. Before long Old Good Eye had made himself at home in Tombstone.

Like always, when I arrived at the high school in Tombstone, I walked down the hall past the home-ec room on my way to the lockers. As I passed the home-ec room I heard Miss Rose, the home-ec teacher, saying, "Good doggie. Good doggie." No dogs were allowed in the building so I looked in the door to see if there really was a dog in there. And sure enough, there was Old Good Eye. Miss Rose had laid frozen fish on the tables to thaw for her first cooking class. She was afraid of this big spotted dog that was rapidly swallowing all the frozen fish. So I grabbed Old Good Eye and escorted him out of the home-ec room, down the hall and out the door before the first bell rang.

I don't know what became of Old Good Eye but I'm sure wherever he went, he was remembered.

The Fifth Foster

Mom had her share of ails and ills. Dad took her to the doctor in Tombstone and he diagnosed her with gall bladder problems. At that time Tombstone had a doctor and a hospital. Mom was put in the hospital and her gall bladder removed. It was quite an operation back then. This improved her health for a while.

Before long she began having digestive trouble again and she looked bloated all the time. She was uncomfortable and sick. So it was back to the doctor. These trips to Tombstone were major undertakings and only done for a serious matter. We didn't know how serious - this would change all our lives.

Mary and I stayed home and worried but when Mom and Dad returned they were in great spirits. Mom was five months pregnant.

Everyone felt protective towards Mom and everyone was sure she couldn't handle a baby at her age. Dad's sister, Jo, came from Texas and stayed with us for the big event. Mary postponed getting married so she would be home to help. The Hunts came too to lend assistance.

Richard made his entrance into our world in November during the fall roundup just four days before his mother's forty second birthday. There were no problems of any kind and he was a beautiful baby.

As luck would have it the wagon was camped at the Wolf Place when all this happened. Dad wrapped Richard in a warm blanket and took him out to the wagon to introduce him to all the cowboys. He told them, "See what I did with a little help from my wife." Dad was fifty three years old.

Aunt Jo went back to Texas, the Hunts went home, the roundup ended, Mary got married and life went back to normal.

The Company brought out a bottle of butane and a hot plate so Mom could heat Richard's bottles at night without having to build a fire. They also brought out a couple of cases of Carnation canned milk for his formula. Boquillas was taking good care of their youngest cowboy.

Mom was generous with Richard. I was allowed to feed, bathe and dress him whenever I wanted but never was I expected to care for him or babysit. The time I spent with him was by my choice only. He was the first baby I had ever been around.

Any time I was in the house I took care of Richard. I took him on his first lizard hunt - you always let the lizard go. I also took him for his first horseback ride. He went with me when I milked the cow in the evenings. He was great company. We were the last Fosters at home.

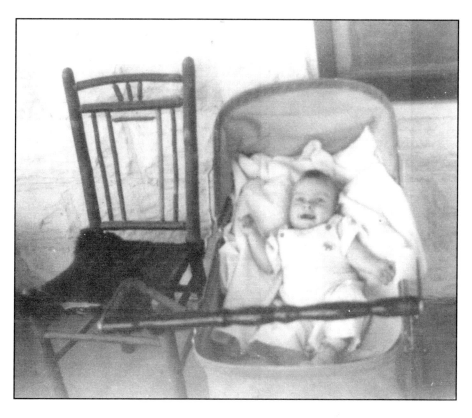

Mesquite chair and Richard in his buggy.

Dad holding Richard on Lupe. The Company brought a butane
hot plate and butane tank for heating Richard's bottles.

The Bobcat

One day when Dad came in from riding he had two bobcat kittens in his shirt. They had just gotten their eyes open. He pulled them out of his shirt and dropped them in the buggy with Richard. As soon as the kittens were in the buggy the fleas started hoping all over the baby. Mom threw a fit. So Dad de-flead the little bobcats before they could be reintroduced to the baby.

A couple of Richard's bottles were donated for the kittens. Dad decided to keep the male and he gave the female to Mom's sister, Ruth, to raise. We called our bobcat Pooky and he loved Richard from the very beginning. He never put out his claws when he played and he always returned any toy he took.

Before long Pooky grew into a good sized cat. It was my job to keep him fed. This meant keeping him in rabbits as he didn't eat cat food like the house cat. In a pinch he would eat home butchered beef but he wouldn't touch store-bought meat. I spent all my free time hunting rabbits with the single shot .22 rifle. I skinned, cleaned and washed the rabbits to get rid of any parasites before bringing them to the house. One jack rabbit made two meals - morning and night - or one cottontail at a feeding. This kept me busy.

One of Pooky's favorite pastimes was stalking the big black and white house cat. He hid behind chair legs and crawled across the open floor and finally pounced. The cat didn't take too kindly to this and it always ended with Pooky getting his ears boxed but it never discouraged him.

Another favorite game of Pooky's was sneaking up behind Mom's rocking chair and jumping up over the back and landing in her lap. So it wasn't long before Dad would seat company in the rocking chair. They would be surprised and startled when suddenly out of nowhere a big warm bobcat landed in their lap.

There was an outbreak of feline distemper that killed most of the cats in the Hereford area. The female bobcat that Ruth had was stricken and died. Ruth was devastated so Dad gave Pooky to her.

The last we heard of Pooky he had made himself at home at Nick's Place and became an attraction running down the bar weaving in and out of the glasses and visiting with the customers.

Pooky, the bobcat kitten, playing in the mesquite chair Dad made.
It had a cow hide seat.

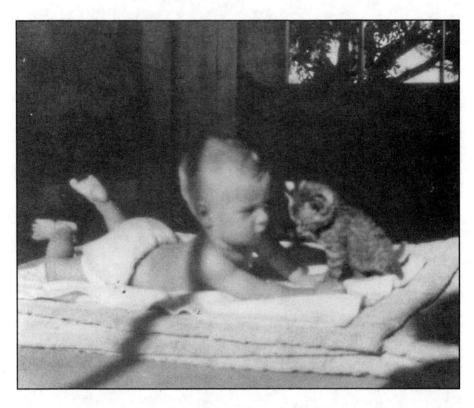

Richard and the bobcat were babies together.

Richard and the bobcat playing.

The bobcat was very gentle playing around Richard.

Carrying Wood

At the other camps the men did the outside work - this included the chores - and the women did the inside work. The women only did the chores if the men were late coming home or were away on roundup. This was how it was - except at our house.

One evening I had finished chopping the wood and was carrying it to the house. The wood pile was under the big cottonwood tree. I would carry as much wood at a time as I could to save making so many trips. There is no way to carry a huge arm load of wood gracefully.

I was so intent on what I was doing I didn't hear a car drive up the road. We had company. I had to cross the road to get to the house. I was in the middle of the road when the car pulled up and had to wait for me to get out of the way.

After they left Dad called me over and told me the next time I was carrying wood, watch the road. If someone was coming drop the wood and get to the house. It seems I had embarrassed Dad. It was alright to do the chores but don't get caught at it.

Cooking for the Roundup

One spring the Company didn't pull the wagon. This meant the woman at each camp would cook for the roundup crew. I only saw this happen once. When the roundup came to the Wolf Place I did the cooking as Mom didn't cook as long as Mary and I were home. Mary had left home the previous fall so it was up to me. I had just turned fourteen. I could handle the cooking but some help with the menu would have been appreciated but Mom left it all up to me.

It was April and it got daylight early. Breakfast had to be over by four in the morning so I got up at two o'clock, built a fire and started cooking. There were about fifteen men and the food was set out on tables in the kitchen. The men served themselves and found a place to sit. The older men usually sat at the table in the dining/living room.

Breakfast was always the same. It consisted of biscuits, milk gravy, steak, pancakes, eggs, bacon, cream of wheat, oatmeal and lots of coffee. As soon as the men left I cleaned the kitchen and started cooking dinner. I was told the men would be in to eat somewhere between eight and eleven o'clock in the morning. If I remember right they came in around eleven o'clock but I had dinner ready early just in case.

As soon as the noon meal was over and the cowboys left again I cleaned the kitchen and started making desserts for supper and dinner the following day. Cowboys liked sweets so I made lots of desserts and a good variety. Supper was always at six o'clock in the evening. After the kitchen was cleaned I was through for the day.

Dad or one of the boys did the outside chores while the roundup was at the house. The roundup was at the house for about a week to ten days.

The Ramuda

When all the horses were put together for roundup, they were called the ramuda. The ramuda consisted of one hundred ten to one hundred twenty head of horses. During roundup each man was given six head of horses for his mount. The horses worked hard and were ridden a half day. After the noon meal each cowboy saddled a fresh horse for the afternoon work. This meant each horse was ridden no more than once every three days.

The ramuda was kept in the horse pasture at night. At first light two cowboys wrangled horses. They were brought into a tight bunch. There were too many horses to fit into the corral so a rope corral was made. Each cowboy held one end of his rope and threw the other end to the next cowboy and so on until a rope corral was made around the horses. This used most but not all the cowboys. There were two ropers. These had to be cowboys who knew every horse by name and who were good ropers. Each cowboy called out the name of the horse he wanted and the roper caught him and led him to the edge of the rope corral where the rope was lowered allowing the horse to be led out. As soon as this cowboy saddled his horse he relieved one of the men holding the ropes so he could saddle his horse when it was caught. Before long all the cowboys had their horses saddled. This could be an interesting time as on a cold morning some of these horses would buck.

The ramuda was driven out of the horse pasture and left in the care of the horse wrangler. He let them graze and kept them in a given area. Then the cowboys rode off to work. They looked like a posse.

The cowboys came in for their noon meal around eleven or twelve o'clock. As soon as someone finished eating he rode out to relieve the horse wrangler so he could come back to the wagon and get something to eat. Then they all rode out to the ramuda and caught fresh horses. When they finished the day's work the ramuda was brought back into the horse pasture for the night.

I loved horses more than anything else. These were good horses that worked hard and knew how to work. They were cow horses. They came in all colors except paint and palomino as the Company didn't like these. These horses weren't pets and they weren't gentle by today's standard. In the evening I was allowed to walk among the ramuda. I had to be escsorted by Dad or one of the boys as it wasn't seemly for a young girl to be out alone. The boys knew most of the horses by name but Dad knew them all and who they belonged to.

It was on one of these walks that Dad told me about the private life of the horse. He had a best friend that he might see only during roundup. Every time the horses were moved the friends became separated. Then as soon as they were free again, bedlam broke out. There were horses running in every direction, whinnying and nickering, trying to find their friend. Of course, there were squeals when a fight broke out. These weren't serious fights as all the horses were geldings. After while all the horses settled down and all was quiet.

I think the horses liked the roundup as it was almost like party time even if they worked hard. It was a wonderful thing to watch. When a horse got older and was no longer able to stand up to the work required of him he was sold, usually out of state because of the wagon rod brand he carried on his left hip. Quite often these horses were bought by small ranchers. They were still good horses with a few years of lighter work left in them.

Once in a while a horse would be condemned for incorrigibility or for health reasons. Boquillas was good about keeping a horse a few years past his normal retirement if a cowboy or his family was particularly fond of him.

Every year new horses were added to the ramuda. They were bought as broncs. The Company bronc rider broke these horses and typically rode them five saddles. By this time they were considered started and ready to be passed on to the camp cowboys. The foreman took first pick, then the bronc rider, and after that each cowboy according to seniority. Each cowboy named his new horse.

Each camp man had six to nine horses. If there was a shortage of horses during roundup he would have to turn in some of his horses. Dad had about fifteen horses so he always had to turn some in. He was allowed extra horses because I rode every day. Boquillas was good to me. While Sammy and Bailey were living at home the Company issued them each four horses and they shared with me. When they left home Dad shared with me.

Between roundups the extra horses were turned out to pasture at the Stone House Camp near St. David. There was a cienega there and good grass year round. If a cowboy was dissatisfied with a horse he could trade for one of the extras.

1952 spring roundup they didn't pull the wagon. This is only part
of the ramuda. Dad is on the right wearing the bat wing chaps.

Horseshoeing

All horses were shod before roundup and after the roundup each cowboy drove his string of horses home.

After the fall roundup Dad pulled the shoes off all the horses and reshod the three he would ride during the winter. The other horses were then turned out of the horse pasture. They could roam wherever they pleased. They were free until they would be brought back in and shod for the spring roundup.

When these horses were brought back into the horse pasture their manes and tails were full of cockle burs and their tails had grown long. We took out the cockle burs and burned them. Then we pulled their tails - a few hair at a time - until their tails were just above their hocks. This was a safety issue as well as getting the horses ready to go back to work.

One of the three horses kept for the winter would be the new bronc. He would be fed and ridden all winter and be ready for the spring roundup in April. He was on his way to being a cow horse.

When horses were being ridden their feet were trimmed and their shoes reset once a month. Most of the horses were good about having their feet worked on but a few had to be hobbled and maybe a hind leg tied to their shoulder.

I always held the horse during shoeing. My job was to hold the horse still and keep him from running over the horse shoer. Of course, it wasn't really necessary as Dad and the boys could do just fine without me. But I was there to look after the horse.

Usually most horses were alright about their front feet. It was their back that could be a problem. When their back foot was picked up they should relax and allow their leg to be extended out behind them and let their foot rest in the horse shoer's lap. However, this didn't always happen. Sometimes a horse kicked or wouldn't allow his leg to be stretched out. Some horses would refuse to peacefully allow their back feet to be shod. When this happened, he was first hobbled, if that didn't work, his back foot was tied to his shoulder and his shoe was put on. It wasn't easy to shoe a horse this way but possible. If he still kicked, he was sidelined. The back foot still on the ground was tied to his front feet. Now if he kicked he would no longer be able to keep his balance and he fell. As soon as he hit the ground he was tied so he couldn't move and he was shod laying down. Some horses grunted and squealed in protest. Usually before a horse was sidelined a twitch would be used and he would allow his back feet to be shod. A twitch is a shortened axe handle with a hole drilled in the small end and a loop of rope running through the hole. This is placed on his upper lip and twisted and his head pushed up in the air. As long as the horse holds still his lip is ok bit if he moves, his lip is in trouble - sort of like twisting someone's arm only worse.

I always wanted to be the one holding the twitch as I thought I might be more gentle. No one likes to use a twitch on a horse but it's a lot easier to shoe a horse standing up than laying down. Most horses learn from the experience and are on good behavior when they are shod the next time. Of course, there are the exceptions. Dad had two such horses - Hippy and Harry Wheeler. Both of these horses were very special to me and were always shod on the ground. They were never peaceful about being shod.

Most cowboys were good horse shoers. When a cowboy shoes a horse he trims off the excess hoof and levels it with a rasp. Then he picks out the right size shoe and using a hammer and anvil the shoe is shaped to fit the hoof. After that the shoe is tacked on using three nails on each side and the protruding nails are twisted off. Then the nails are clenched so the shoes will stay on.

I was fifteen when I decided I really wanted to shoe a horse. It took some talking to persuade Dad to let me try. It was decided that I would shoe a brown horse named Shady. He was an older horse with lots of patience. All went well and when I finished Dad had me reward Shady with a moral full of oats even though it was in the summer. Then I took his picture.

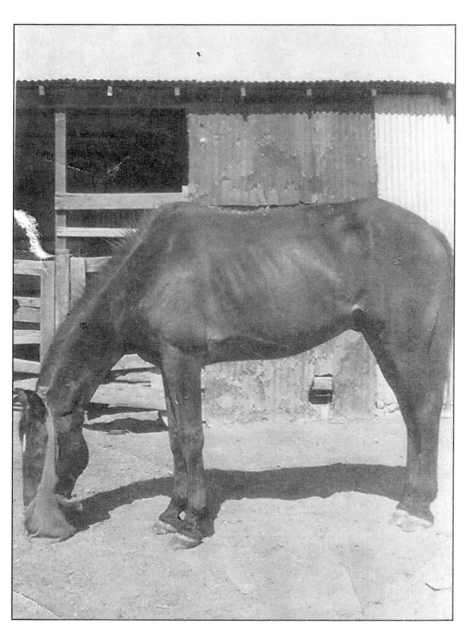

Shady after dad let me shoe him.

Roundup

Roundup came twice a year. The chuck wagon and team of mules had been replaced with a more modern version but it was still called the chuck wagon. The chuck wagon was now a big red bob-tail truck with racks on the sides. This was the pantry.

The campfire had been replaced with a wood cook stove with the warming oven removed. It had a steel table hinged on the end that folded over the top of the stove for traveling. The stove itself sat on an axle with two tires and had a tongue so it could be hooked on behind the truck. There was even a barrel mounted behind the stove for a wood box.

When camp was set up the stove was unhooked and turned around with the front of the stove facing the back of the truck. There was a large wooden chuck box on the back of the truck. It had a door that hinged down and made a work surface for the cook. This was his kitchen. The cook's helper was called a flunky. He chopped wood and kept the wood box full, carried water, did the dishes and helped the cook.

There was a big white tent about twenty by sixty feet that was attached to the truck and provided a large place for everyone to eat and sleep if they wished. Typically the roundup crew consisted of at least fifteen men. Some of the older cowboys had teepees that they slept in. These were not provided by the Company but were personally owned. Dad bought his teepee from Sears Roebuck and waterproofed it with green paint. All the other teepees were white.

The cowboys always rolled up their bedrolls when they got up in the morning. On moving day everyone helped drop the big tent, roll it up and load it. The cook and flunky took the truck loaded with the tent, bedrolls and teepees to the next camp site with the stove hooked on behind the truck. With the use of the truck the cook and flunky could set up the big tent and have dinner ready when the cowboys came in to eat.

The spring roundup started around the first of April and lasted about a month. All calves were born about a month before spring roundup. The purpose of the spring roundup was to brand, ear mark, vaccinate, castrate the bull calves and get a tally on how many calves there were. Each calf was branded with the wagon rod - Ó Ọ - on the left shoulder and hip. The heifer calves had the last number of the year branded on their jaw. Then if they were used for replacement heifers it was easy to keep track of their age.

The fall roundup started in the middle of October. On the fall roundup all the calves were shipped so the mother cows had no nursing calves during the winter. This took care of weaning the calves. Any cow with the last number of the current year on her jaw was also shipped. She was ten years old and her best productive years were behind her. This was when the herd was culled. All old, sick or cancer-eyed cows were shipped.

During roundup when they were camped under the big tree, we took our meals at the wagon except for breakfast. Dad would come to the house and escort us out to the big tent. We ate out of enamelware plates or metal pie tins like the cowboys. We sat on bedrolls for chairs. When we finished eating we put our dishes in a wash tub filled with hot soapy water. The food was hearty, delicious and plentiful. As a thank you for our meals we supplied the desserts.

Dad was usually home for Thanksgiving and it was time to settle in for the winter.

The chuck wagon. Dad's teepee is in the foreground.

Inside the chuck wagon. Clyde Allen is cooking supper.

Clyde Allen is cutting meat for supper and the flunky is peeling
potatoes. The stove hooked on behind the truck when
they moved camp and the table folded over the stove.
The wash tubs on the ground are the dish pans.

Dad standing by the tent at the chuck wagon.

The chuck wagon. Leo McKinney, general manager, Joe Kitchen, foreman, Clyde Allen, Cook, and Dad holding his horse Doc.

Screw Worms

Screw worms were the larva of the blow fly. The female blow fly didn't lay eggs. She laid living maggots - screw worms - into an open wound of a living animal. These tiny maggots soon became large screw worms that fed on living flesh. Left unchecked they killed their host. Wormy season lasted from spring until fall.

I've heard it said that the Longhorn cattle would submerge their bodies in the water for long periods of time and drown these parasites. I don't know if domesticated cattle did this too but the Hereford cattle on Boquillas had no deep water available to them so they were dependent on human help.

Dad cut the tops off an old pair of boots and made two pouches that he fastened on each side of his saddle behind the cantle. In one pouch he carried a pint of black Peerless screw worm medicine. Peerless also came in clear pink but Dad felt that the black tarry version was more effective. In the other pouch he carried dry horse manure. He preferred this to cotton.

All the calves were born in early spring before the spring roundup began. Many of these calves got screw worms in their navels and where their brands peeled during the healing process. Adult cattle also got screw worms if there was any place on their bodies where blood was drawn - even a small scratch. There were a lot of adult cattle that were infected with screw worms.

When a calf had screw worms he was roped and doctored then black smear was rubbed into his white forehead. That way when you saw a calf with a black spot on his forehead he could be checked to be sure he was healed or needed to be doctored again. This black smear also colored the white flank of the mother cow when her calf nursed. So if you saw a cow with a black flank, you knew she had a wormy calf and he had to found and looked at.

If it was decided that an animal needed to be doctored more than once, they were put into a "hospital". One was at Snake Flat where there was a small pasture with an artesian water trough, another was at the house in the horse trap and the third at Lewis Springs in a pasture that had a flowing spring for a water source. These "hospitals" were doctored every other day. As each animal healed they were released.

You rode north one day and south the next checking every cow and calf you found. At the Wolf Place there were about three hundred head of mother cows with calves and thirty bulls.

We left the house after breakfast and rode until noon. Then we doctored a "hospital" before coming home for dinner. Before we came in to eat we wrangled horses. After dinner we saddled a fresh horse and rode until chore time.

When it was just Dad and I, he roped the calves by the head and I flanked them. With the cows, he caught both hind feet and I tailed them down. If a bull needed to be doctored Dad roped both back feet and rode around and around him pulling the rope tight until all four feet were together and then he could be pulled over.

Normally when we rode when there weren't screw worms, we left the house after breakfast and stayed out until about two o'clock. This gave us at least a seven hour day. Dad didn't believe in carrying food or water. We drank out of the river but during flood season you waited until you got home to get a drink. The same was true for food, you waited until you got home. When Mary was home she would have dinner ready when we got there. After she left, I cooked dinner when I got in from riding.

Dad rode seven days a week but he did get two weeks vacation every summer.

When an animal was doctored the wound was filled with Peerless and then cotton or dried horse manure packed on top to seal out the air. After waiting about five to ten minutes the packing was removed and the dead screw worms cleaned out. Then more peerless was put into the wound and the animal released. If any bleeding occurred they would be reinfected. The Peerless helped form a scab while healing. One of the active ingredients in Peerless was chloroform.

Then around 1953, the government flew over the ranches and dropped male blow flies that had been sterilized with radiation.

These sterile male blow flies mated with the females and no larva was produced. All ranches were given tubes packed inside a cardboard cylinder complete with postage and label. If a case of screw worms were found you sent in the location and a sample of the larva. Then another drop of sterilized flies was made in this area.

The cases of screw worms sharply declined and in a short time the screw worm had been eradicated.

Feeding Cattle

The Company fed the cows during the winter. They were fed cottonseed pellets which were high in protein. They also had good pasture but these cows were carrying next spring's calves and they needed the extra nourishment.

The red bob-tail truck would deliver a load of one-hundred pound sacks of cottonseed pellets to each camp. Then the cowboy hitched the mules to the wagon and loaded it with as many sacks as the wagon would hold and the mules could pull. The feed was unloaded in "cake houses". These were small tin houses about the size of an outhouse. This kept the feed dry and secure.

When the feed had been distributed it was time to start feeding the cattle. Dad rode north one day and south the next feeding cows. As soon as he left the horse pasture he began calling cattle. They came out of the mesquite thickets and began following the rider on horseback. When a cake house was reached about a third of a sack of feed was shaken out on the ground. It was spread out so all the cows could eat without too much pushing and shoving. Then it was on to the next cake house. There were cake houses on both sides of the river and about a mile apart. As soon as the last cake house was reached it was time to head home and repeat the process in the other direction the next day.

We were in school during the winter but on weekends Dad let us go with him to feed. There were only three horses so the boys went most of the time but Dad made time for me too.

I loved feeding cattle and I was allowed to grab the gunny sack and make a run for it while shaking the cottonseed pellets out on the ground. These cattle were hungry and greedy and they almost ran over the person doing the feeding.

Feeding cattle and wrangling horses were definitely my favorite things to do.

Richard and Shep 1954

Richard on the back steps of Wolf Place.

The Butane Water Heater

The Company modernized in 1954. The wood cook stove and galvanized hot water were replaced with a Servel butane kitchen range and water heater. They even brought a Servel refrigerator. These were beautiful top of the line appliances. We had really come up in the world. We still had the wood heater in the livingroom that we used for heat. So that meant there was still wood to chop - but not as much.

This was a whole new way of life. There were pilot lights on everything so there was no need for matches but I never gave up carrying matches in my pocket. You never knew when you might need a match.

There was a big new butane tank outside of the yard fence on the east side of the house. I loved the old wood stove and I would miss it but this was nice.

But soon there was a problem. The pilot light went out on the new water heater. First Dad tried to light it but it wouldn't stay lit. Then it was Mom's turn. They each read the directions and took turns trying to get the pilot light to stay lit. I came along confident that I could read and follow the directions clearly printed on the front of the water heater.

Dad had decided I should look and behave a little more like a lady. Mom gave me one of her silky housecoats. So after I had milked the cow, wrangled horses, cooked breakfast and cleaned the kitchen, I was to spend the morning lounging in this rose colored rayon-acetate full length house coat. It was smooth, silky and gorgeous. I have to admit I felt very pretty in it.

I had a logical mind and I was confident that if the directions were followed exactly, the pilot light would stay lit and all would be well. After all, this was a new appliance that had been inspected at the factory and had been installed by a professional. It had worked for a while. Of course, the mystery of why the pilot light went out in the first place was never solved or given too much thought.

I was also confident that I could read the directions clearly printed above the door on the tank, follow these directions precisely and achieve success. The kitchen cabinets ran along the east wall and ended short of the corner leaving just enough room for the water heater. The new stove sat on the kitchen's north wall about a foot and a half from the cabinets. This gave a narrow access back into the corner to the water heater.

I definitely was not dressed appropriately for this type of chore but at least the floor was clean. I laid face down on the floor and worked my way back into the corner. The directions on the tank were short and clear. To the best of my recollection, they went something like this: " Hold down the red button. Light the pilot light. Continue holding the red button until it clicked. Release the red button and the pilot light would remain on." How hard could that be?

I was propped up on my elbows, laying on my stomach, stretched full length on the kitchen floor and still wearing the silky rose colored housecoat. I followed the directions exactly. I was holding down the red button waiting for it to click when I very clearly heard a voice tell me to get out of there. The water heater was going to blow up.

I put the palms of my hands on the floor and started pushing myself out of the corner as fast as I could - but I was not fast enough. I did succeed in getting about two feet back from the water heater when there was a loud "WHOOM".

After it was over and the damage assessed, this is the best account I can give of what happened. The fire ball hit my hands and face and rolled over my head. Then it bounced and landed on the back of my legs just above my ankles.

My hands and arms were burned the worst. My long fingernails were melted and curled back on the nail bed. They had melted down to the quick. They were too hard for an emery board or nail file to be effective. I took a razor blade and carefully cut off my nails. My face was burned deep enough to blister but when I healed there were no scars. I did have some scarring on one hand. The part that bothered me the most was my hair. I had no eyelashes or eyebrows and I had lost about an inch of my hairline from ear to ear. My hair was long enough to sit on and I kept it braided in a single braid, tucked under and pinned to my head. That was probably the only thing that kept me from losing all of my hair and possibly catching on fire.

The strangest thing was that there was a perfect imprint of the water heater door melted out of the lower edge of the pretty rose colored housecoat just above my ankles.

This happened in the early part of the summer so by the time school started I had healed and grown back my eyelashes and eyebrows. It would take longer to grow back my hair and have a normal hairline.

If I hadn't pushed myself back from the water heater I would have been burned much worse. I do believe a guardian angel looked after me that day. And I also believe I wasn't meant to wear beautiful long silky housecoats and lounge around the house.

Dad and Mom standing in front of the lily pond.

Top row: Dad and Mom. Middle row: Bailey, Betty, Lowrie
O'Donnell, Mary Foster O'Donnell and Sammy.
Bottom row: Richard, Marion O'Donnell, and Ramona O' Donnell.

Leaving Home

My high school friend gave two newly hatched ugly baby birds. She insisted they were orioles because they had been rescued from an oriole nest after a summer storm blew down the cottonwood tree holding their nest. I didn't know what kind of birds they were at the time, but I was certain they weren't orioles. No baby bird is pretty when it is first hatched but these birds were truly ugly with their dark reddish skins, large triangular heads and big feet.

Surprisingly, one of these little birds lived, grew feathers and became a handsome bird. He was a bronzed cowbird with red eyes and a heavy bill - very common in the area. We called them blackbirds. I tried to reintroduce him into the wild but he wanted no part of it. He was content to be a house bird. I even took him out with me when I did the milking and he hopped along the cow's back and caught flies. But when I went back to the house he wasn't going to be left behind. I had a bird. Tito.

The section foreman's daughter down at Lewis Springs had a cat that had kittens. She told me I could have my pick of the litter. Just what I needed. I had a real soft spot for yellow cats so I picked out a deep orange kitten with short hair and named him Toby. My dependents were growing. I don't remember where the goldfish came from but I had two of them.

At the end of my seventeenth summer, Charlie and I went to the courthouse in Bisbee and were married by Judge Thomas. We went back by the Wolf Place and picked up my things. I didn't have much. I only had a few clothes, a box of books and my saddle. And, of course, my "livestock" - a blackbird, an orange kitten and two goldfish. I said my goodbyes and departed.

I didn't get an education or become a teacher like I had planned. But I did find happiness and became a wife and mother.

And so it was that on August 1, 1955, my first life ended and my second life began. Life was good.

Remedies

Baby with colic - A spoonful of warm milk with cigarette smoke blown across it to put nicotine in the milk.

Earache - Blow warm cigarette smoke into the ear.

Pacifier - (Sugar Tit) - A small piece of cloth folded around a spoonful of sugar and dipped in water.

Eyewash - Diluted salt water.

Rusty nail - Soak in either kerosene or turpentine.

Cuts - Wrap in clean cloth in it's own blood.

Warts - Slice off the end of the wart with sharp knife or razor blade just deep enough to draw blood. Dip a toothpick in the blood and use this to pick up a flake of lye. The lye will stick to the blood. Put the lye on the wart until the blood turns black. Remove the lye and let heal. The wart will be gone.

Deep thorns - Poultice made from peeled prickly pear leaf. (I had a thorn in my foot that went straight in and deep and couldn't be dug out. Mrs. Bakarich took a prickly pear and removed the skin and thorns. She placed this on my foot and wrapped it up. The next morning the thorn had been drawn out.

For almost everything else let nature take it's course. Nature is a wonderful healer. There were very few times we needed the services of a doctor.

WORDS OF WISDOM

Be a laborer great or small,
Do it well or not at all.
When a job is once begun,
Never leave it 'til it's done.

Fool's names are like monkey's faces.
Always seen in public places.

Willful waste makes woeful want.

Eat it up. Wear it out.
Use it up or do without.

A place for everything and everything in it's place.

A stitch in time - saves nine.

Never put off until tomorrow what you can do today.

It's better to be thought a fool than to open your mouth
and remove all doubt.

Love is like lightning. It is as likely to strike an outhouse
as it is to strike a mansion.

He who cries the loudest has the most to hide.

Live life like an open book and you will have nothing to fear.

If you don't want to do something - don't think about it.
If you think about it long enough - you will do it.

Every day a boy spends in school dulls
his natural ability to trail a cow.

Let a boy in the house and you'll ruin him.

One boy is a boy.
Two boys are half a boy.
Three boys are no boy at all.

If wishes were horses - Beggars would ride.

An ounce of prevention is worth a pound of cure.

A bird in the hand is worth two in the bush.

Pretty is as pretty does.

Pride goeth before a fall.

A pint's a pound, the world around.

Dad told us kids when he died he couldn't leave us anything
except the knowledge of hard work - and that he did. He couldn't
have left us a greater gift.